How to Measure Attitudes

Marlene E. Henerson
Lynn Lyons Morris
Carol Taylor Fitz-Gibbon

Center for the Study of Evaluation
University of California, Los Angeles

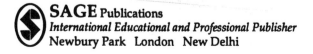

SAGE Publications
International Educational and Professional Publisher
Newbury Park   London   New Delhi

The second edition of the *Program Evaluation Kit* was developed at the Center for the Study of Evaluation, Graduate School of Education, University of California, Los Angeles.

The development of this second edition of the CSE *Program Evaluation Kit* was supported in part by a grant from the National Institute of Education, currently known as the Office of Educational Research and Improvement. However, the opinions expressed herein do not necessarily reflect the position or policy of that agency and no official endorsement should be inferred.

The second edition of the *Program Evaluation Kit* is published and distributed by Sage Publications, Inc., Newbury Park, California, under an exclusive agreement with The Regents of the University of California.

For information address:

 SAGE Publications, Inc.
2455 Teller Road
Newbury Park, California 91320

SAGE Publications Ltd.
6 Bonhill Street
London EC2A 4PU
United Kingdom

SAGE Publications India Pvt. Ltd.
M-32 Market
Greater Kailash I
New Delhi 110 048 India

Printed in the United States of America

Library of Congress Cataloging-in-Publication Data

Henerson, Marlene E.
    How to measure attitudes / Marlene E. Henerson, Lynn Lyons Morris,
Carol Taylor Fitz-Gibbon. --2nd ed.
        p. cm. -- (Program evaluation kit ; 6)
        "Developed at the Center for the Study of Evaluation, Graduate
School of Education, University of California, Los Angeles."—T.p.
verso.
        Bibliography: p.
        Includes index.
        ISBN 0-8039-3131-X (pbk.)
        1. Attitude (Psychology)—Testing.   I. Morris, Lynn Lyons.
II. Fitz-Gibbon, Carol Taylor.   III. University of California, Los
Angeles. Center for the Study of Evaluation.   IV. Title.
V. Series: Program evaluation kit (2nd ed.) ; 6.
BF327.H46   1987
152.4'52'0287--dc19   87-16982   **94 15 14 13**
                    CIP

Contents

Acknowledgments

The preparation of this second edition of the Center for the Study of Evaluation *Program Evaluation Kit* has been a challenging task, made possible only through the combined efforts of a number of individuals.

First and foremost, Drs. Lynn Lyons Morris and Carol Taylor Fitz-Gibbon, the authors and editor of the original Kit. Together, they authored all eight of the original volumes, an enormous undertaking that required incredible knowledge, dedication, persistence, and painstaking effort. Lynn also worked relentlessly as editor of the entire set. Having struggled through only a revision, I stand in great awe of Lynn's and Carol's enormous accomplishment. This second edition retains much of their work and obviously would not have been possible without them.

Thanks also are due to Gene V Glass, Ernie House, Michael Q. Patton, Carol Weiss, and Robert Boruch, who reviewed our plans and offered specific assistance in targeting needed revisions. The work would not have proceeded without Marvin C. Alkin, who planted the seeds for the second edition and collaborated very closely during the initial planning phases.

I would like to acknowledge especially the contribution and help of Michael Q. Patton. True to form, Michael was an excellent, utilization-focused formative evaluator for the final draft manuscript, carefully responding to our work and offering innumerable specific suggestions for its improvement. We have incorporated into the *Handbook* his framework for differentiating among kinds of evaluation studies (formative, summative, implementation, outcomes).

Many staff members at the Center for the Study of Evaluation contributed to the production of the Kit. The entire effort was supervised by Aeri Lee, able office manager at the Center. Katherine Fry, word processing expert, was able to accomplish incredible graphic feats for the *Handbook* and tirelessly labored on manuscript production and data transfer. Ruth Paysen, who was a major contributor to the production of the original Kit, also was a painstaking and dedicated proofreader for the second edition. Margie Franco, Tori Gouveia, and Katherine Lu also participated in the production effort.

Marie Freeman and Pamela Aschbacher, also from the Center, contributed their ideas, editorial skills, and endless examples. Carli

Rogers, of UCLA Contracts and Grants, was both caring and careful in her negotiations for us.

At Sage Publications, thanks to Sara McCune for her encouragement and to Mitch Allen for his nudging and patience.

And at the Center for the Study of Evaluation, the project surely would not have been possible without Eva L. Baker, Director. Eva is a continuing source of encouragement, ideas, support, fun, and friendship.

—Joan L. Herman
Center for the Study of Evaluation
University of California, Los Angeles

Chapter 1

An Introduction to the Measurement of Attitudes and Attitude Change

This book should help you develop basic skills in designing and using instruments for the measurement of what are usually referred to as *affective objectives* or *attitudes*. The book's contents are based on the experience of evaluators at the Center for the Study of Evaluation, University of California, Los Angeles, on advice from experts in the field of educational measurement, and on the comments of people in school settings who used a field test edition.

Whenever possible, the book recommends procedures, rules of thumb, and practical, strategies for performing evaluation tasks related to the assessment of peoples' attitudes. Keep in mind that many of the recommended procedures are methods for designing and administering these instruments *under advantageous circumstances*. Few evaluation situations, of course, exactly match those envisioned here, so *you should not expect to be able to duplicate exactly the suggestions in the book*. It is hoped that you will examine the principles and examples provided, and adapt them to the press of your own time constraints and data requirements.

Evaluation is a relatively new field. Few procedures for accomplishing evaluation are hard and fast. The task of any evaluator is to provide the best possible information to program funders, staff, and others with a stake in program processes and outcomes. Your obligation, therefore, is to gather the most highly credible information possible within the constraints of your situation, and to present your conclusion to each evaluation audience in a form that is useful to them.

The *Program Evaluation Kit,* of which this booklet is one component, is intended for use primarily by people who have been assigned to the role of *program evaluator.* Your job as an evaluator will take one of two shapes, and perhaps at times both, depending on the task you have been assigned:

1. You may have responsibility for producing a *summary statement* about the effectiveness of the program. In this case, you probably will report to a funding agency, governmental office, or some other representative of the program's constituency. You may be expected to describe the

program, to produce a statement concerning the program's achievement of announced goals, to note any unanticipated outcomes, and possibly to make comparisons with alternative programs. If these are the features of your job, you are a *summative evaluator.*

2. Your evaluation task may characterize you as a *helper* and *advisor* to the program planners and developers. You may then be called on to look out for potential problems, identify areas where the program needs improvement, describe and monitor program activities, and periodically test for progress in achievement or attitude change. In this situation, you are a "jack of all trades," a person whose overall task is not well defined. You may or may not be required to produce a report at the end of your activities. If this more loosely defined job role seems closer to yours, then you are a *formative evaluator.*

Most of the information about the design of attitude measures contained in this booklet will be useful for both formative and summative tasks. Your perspective on the measurement of attitude outcomes will vary, however, depending on which of the two roles is yours.

The *summative* evaluator will be interested mainly in finding and using instruments to measure attainment of *overall goals* of the program. For this reason, the summative evaluator will pay close attention to the program's announced attitude objectives and will be interested in designing attitude measures which are sensitive to measuring their possible achievement. In addition, the summative evaluator may be concerned with measuring attitudes which the program designers *have not mentioned* among their objectives, but which seem to the evaluator important for describing the program's overall impact.

Because the summative evaluator must produce a report which could affect important decisions about the program's future, he will be interested in ensuring *high credibility* in the instruments he produces or chooses to use. The summative evaluator, then, must opt for high validity and reliability. The evaluator producing a summary report may be called upon to defend conclusions based on measurements. When describing the results of programs which place great emphasis on the achievement of attitude objectives, this need for good credibility will require the summative evaluator to find *multiple indicators* of the degree to which attitudinal ambitions were realized.

The *formative* evaluator will be able to measure attitudes less formally. The audience for the information which the formative evaluator produces is the program staff and planners. Staff members, because they are working close to the program themselves, will usually not demand high instrument validity and reliability. Besides, the formative evaluator's reason for measuring attitudes will be less official than the summative evaluator's. The formative evaluator produces informal measures to make *progress checks* throughout the course of the program, or to use as pre- and posttests for short experiments to try out new program components. Because of these less rigid data collection requirements, the formative evaluator can usually take greater risks and be more creative in the design and choice of attitude instruments. Of course, if the formative evaluator finds himself producing measurements to settle controversies among the staff about various best ways to implement the program, the need for credible results will again become critical.

An incidental aim of the formative evaluator should be to find or produce well conceived instruments which are sensitive measures of the program's effects. These can influence the content of the instruments which eventually will be used for summative evaluation of the program. The formative evaluator, in addition, may aim data collection toward *encouraging dialogue* about the program. For this reason, he may wish to measure attitudes which are not the expressed aims of the program planners. The formative evaluator's strongest contribution to the program may turn out to be the uncovering of attitudes which the program produced but which had not been planned.

It is possible—and a good idea—to collect attitude information even in the case of programs which have *no* affective goals. Every program, after all, produces attitudes. Even if questions are limited to students' impressions of the quality of the textbook, attitudinal information is usually valuable to both program planners and funders. Attitude measures for purely cognitive programs can be as simple as a single open-ended question asking for comments about how the program is going. In cases where findings from this informal check produce information that will affect interpretation of the program's achievement results, however, the design of a follow-up instrument with high credibility might be necessary.

Whatever your reasons for reading this book, it should acquaint you with the major issues and tasks surrounding the design and use of attitude instruments. Should you wish to explore attitude measurement in greater depth, you will find suggestions for further reading at the end of most chapters.

Problems Unique to Measuring Attitudes

The task of measuring attitudes is not a simple one. What's more, attempting to demonstrate attitude *change,* as some evaluations require, is probably the most difficult of all evaluation tasks. Why is this so?

To begin with, the concept of attitude, like many abstract concepts, is a creation—a construct. As such, it is a tool that serves the human need to see order and consistency in what people say, think and do, so that given certain behaviors, predictions can be made about future behaviors. An attitude is not something we can examine and measure in the same way we can examine the cells of a person's skin or measure the rate of her heartbeat. *We can only infer that a person has attitudes by her words and actions.*

John, for example, says he hates school—that it's a waste of time. He seldom completes an assignment or participates willingly in class activities. He has run-ins with teachers and is frequently truant. We infer a relationship among all these behaviors, and we describe that relationship by saying that John has a *poor attitude toward school.* We then make various predictions from these behaviors, among them, that John will cease to go to school just as soon as he is free to make that decision.

Unfortunately for our measurement purposes, patterns of behavior are not always as consistent as the pattern depicted for John. We know that behavior is the result of many complex factors—feelings engendered by previous experiences, assessments of the expectations of others, anticipation of the consequences of a particular act.

William, like John, says he doesn't care much for school—that it's boring. He is delighted to stay home on any likely pretext. At school, however, he completes all his assignments, has good relationships with his teachers, and is progressing academically. How do we describe *his* attitude toward school? Do we go by what he says? Do we go by what he does at home? At school?

If we go by what he says and if our measure is a questionnaire asking, "Do you like school?" William might score low. If it is his teacher's assessment of William's classroom behavior, he will score high. How can we decide about his true attitude, and on what basis can we say that one of these measures is more valid than the other?

Should we assume that we can accept a person's statements about his own attitude as the best indicator of the attitude? In some instances, yes, particularly when we can see no reason for him to hide anything. If we want to know which series of brown bag lunch discussions the students enjoyed and which ones they disliked, a few straightforward questions should provide us with accurate information. Many of the things we want to know, however, are not so easy to find out.

As a case in point, consider an attitude questionnaire attempting to measure racial prejudice. Mary's responses to the questionnaire indicate one thing; her behavior on the job with people of other races indicates quite another. What is more, her responses to other measures change with the occasion. On Monday, Mary says she loves work. Asked again on Wednesday, she says she doesn't like it much. And don't forget William. If we gauge his attitude toward school by both his own statements and the teacher's report, we have inconsistent information.

When we attempt to measure a complex attitude, as for example, attitude toward school or work, we find that it has many *facets*—feelings and beliefs about one's teachers or supervisors, classmates or co-workers, school subjects or jobs and activities. We find it has many *manifestations*—productivity, attention, interaction with others, verbal responses. When we attempt to measure an attitude such as racial prejudice, we find it is blurred by peer group pressures, the desire to please, ambivalence, inconsistency, lack of self-awareness.

Yet, surely it is complex attitudes like these that we are most interested in influencing and, for evaluation purposes, measuring. We should not back off just because the task is a difficult one; but we should proceed with the following precautions firmly in mind:

- When we measure attitudes, we must rely on *inference,* since it is impossible to measure attitudes directly.
- Behaviors, beliefs, and feelings will not always match, even when we correctly assume that they reflect a single attitude; so to focus on only one manifestation of an attitude may tend to distort our picture of the situation and mislead us.
- We have no guarantee that the attitude we want to assess will "stand still" long enough for a one-time measurement to be reliable. A volatile or fluctuating attitude cannot be revealed by information gathered on one occasion.
- When we study certain attitudes, we do so without universal agreement on their nature. Is there, for instance, such a thing as a single "self-concept"? Perhaps, but perhaps not.

Fortunately, the task of a program evaluator will not usually be to make judgments about the attitudes and feelings of *individuals.* Attitude measurement for program evaluation generally calls for assessment of the attitudes of a *group* of people (e.g., students, teachers, employees, clients, consumers). Though the measures you use must be sensitive to the attitudes you are attempting to measure, they will not need the precision of measurement that is essential for making predictions about individuals.

In this book, the word "attitude" will be used quite broadly to describe all the objectives we want to measure that have to do with affect, feelings, values, or beliefs. It is hoped that this book can help you to decide on the information you need, and to select or develop tools for obtaining that information. Your task may be as simple as determining satisfaction with a set of books, or as complicated as measuring change in racial attitudes. Most likely, even if the evaluation task cannot claim great precision or exactness, it can be done well enough to help people make informed decisions.

Chapter 2

Essential Preliminary Questions

You are planning tò measure attitudes either because the audience[1] for your evaluation will want to know about certain attitudes or because the program you are evaluating is concerned with attitudes. In the latter case, there exist written or unwritten attitude *objectives*. Before you make any decisions about how you will collect attitude information, you should examine your attitude objectives in light of the following five questions, each of which raises issues that must be considered before you proceed.

1. How important are the attitude objectives? Are they the major program objectives, or are they a minor component of the evaluation?

Your answer to this question will determine the quantity and variety of information to be gathered.

Let us say that you, a formative evaluator, are simply interested in an informal assessment of a program's acceptance for the purpose of spotting potential problem areas. You might then decide that a single questionnaire can do the job. If, on the other hand, your task is summative, and major program objectives are attitude objectives, and if there is a likelihood that the program will be dropped should your measure fail to demonstrate growth or change, *you cannot in good conscience depend on just one measure.*

Gauge the importance of an objective by finding out *beforehand* what kinds of decisions depend on evaluation results, and then proceed with the following in mind:

- The more influence your findings will have on important program decisions, the greater the need for a variety of measures.
- Conversely, there is no point in collecting data that will have little or no influence.

2. Are the attitude objectives specific—narrowly defined and described in detail, or are they general—broadly defined and open to alternative interpretations?

Your answer to this question will determine how much time and effort must be spent clarifying the objectives so that they can be measured.

For example, you may be confronted with a very general goal or objective, such as this one:

We hope that Program X will improve pupils' attitudes toward school.

Or a goal or objective stated somewhat more specifically, such as this one:

We hope that Program X will cause the pupils to feel good about their school experiences and the people associated with the school and to perceive their classroom activities as being enjoyable and relevant.

Or a goal or objective described in great detail, such as this one:

We hope that Program X will improve pupils' attitudes toward school. By this we mean that we hope to see some tangible schoolwide changes, among them: (1) a decrease in the defacement of school property, (2) an improvement in the cleanliness of the school, (3) an increase in participation in student government, and (4) an improvement of scores on a school attitude questionnaire.

The people who wrote the most detailed objective have in essence said, "From the many behaviors and reports which could indicate students' attitudes to school, we have selected a few that are of particular interest to us. We feel that these kinds of changes will convince us that the program has had an impact on students' attitudes toward school."

Your first step should be to make sure that the objectives are clear and described in detail and that the program planners and those who will receive the results agree about:

- The major objectives of the program
- The evidence they will accept of their attainment
- The priority of the objectives (if possible)

Reaching agreement on these matters at the beginning of the evaluation will save you from the comment, "Your report is well and good, but since we don't agree with the basic assumptions which *you* made without consulting us, we cannot accept the findings."[2]

3. Can you realistically expect that the attitude objectives will have been achieved by the time you plan to do the measuring?

Your answer to this question will determine to what degree you must focus on the processes (activities, materials) of the program in your evaluation as opposed to the results or outcomes of the program.

For example, many advocates of open classroom instruction maintain that while students in open classrooms may not in any one semester learn more than their counterparts in traditional classrooms, their learning will *eventually* become more self-directed and their total enjoyment of the learning process will be less dependent on the teacher of the moment. Evaluating such a program presents a dilemma: for purposes of evaluation, "eventually" is too long to wait; but holding the program accountable for having a strong immediate effect would be unfair.

Many business programs may also be expected to ultimately influence the attitudes of employees, customers, or clients without having a strong immediate effect. For example, a training program on managing interpersonal relationships would be expected to help some managers alter their behavior over time, and eventually such changes would be expected to result in greater job satisfaction among employees under those managers. It would be unrealistic in such a case to expect an immediate, strong effect.

Should you be in the position of having to evaluate a program with objectives that are either

- unmeasurable (e.g., "The student will develop a lifelong love of learning"), or
- not measurable at the time of the evaluation (e.g., "By the time students reach the upper grades, their intrinsic motivation will have increased; they will have developed an approach to learning which involves the selection of their own learning objectives, the planning of their own instructional activities, and the evaluation of their own performance"),

you might decide to shift the major emphasis of your evaluation from outcomes to processes. This will require that you design a portion of the evaluation to determine whether the classroom instruction adequately reflects the *theory* upon which the program is based. The rationale for this shift in emphasis is a simple one. Money and effort have been invested in the program because people believe that the activities and materials which it includes will cause the development of certain attitudes. The best use of your time as evaluator will be to monitor whether the program looks and operates as it is supposed to. If you are a summative evaluator, you will tell the funding source whether it got what it paid for. If your function is primarily formative, then you will provide information for keeping the program on track. When you decide to focus on process, the questions you ask about the program will shift from, "Did the program promote the desired attitude?" to "Did the program contain the materials and activities it was supposed to?" You should consult with your evaluation audience before deciding on such a course of action.

Please note that an emphasis on process does not mean you should necessarily ignore outcomes. You might want to assess attitudes just to see if you can detect any appreciable change, or to try out your instruments. If you will be evaluating the program over a long period, say, two or three years, an excellent idea is to collect attitude information to use for noting changes in the same group or across grade levels over time. Besides, after a few years you should start to see effects. In this case, it will become essential that you measure attitudes. By this time, the program can be looked upon as a test of whether the activities you have so carefully monitored do indeed bring about the desired attitudes.

4. Are there any ethical or legal problems involved in measuring your attitude objectives?

Your answer to this question will lead you, in certain cases, to obtain permission to use certain measures. In other cases, you may have to give up hope of collecting some kinds of information because of insurmountable legal or ethical problems.

Once you have determined what kind of information you need, it would be wise to consider the legality and ethics of potential information-collection methods. Some states have laws prohibiting the use of "personality tests" in the schools. A "homemade" questionnaire attempting to assess growth in self-esteem could very easily be interpreted by some to fall into the category of a personality test. You certainly don't wish to spend time and energy constructing an evaluation instrument only to find that there is a law or school code prohibiting its use. One large school district in California reported that its administrators have been instructed to proceed with great caution in the area of attitude assessment, since they are required to follow three (sometimes conflicting) guidelines—the recent federal "right-to-privacy" law, the state code, and district policy.

Certain types of measurement devices pose special ethical problems.[3] For example, a sociometric device that asks students or employees to rate one another can have adverse effects on those who are publicly identified as unpopular when the participants discuss their responses among themselves. A questionnaire that purports to seek one kind of information while in fact seeking another may be regarded as unethical and, in the long run, may do your evaluation more harm than good if people discover they were deceived.

Another ethical concern has to do with the confidentiality of the information to be obtained. Whenever possible, you should arrange for the respondents to a questionnaire or the subjects of an observation to remain anonymous. If such anonymity is not feasible, devise a code system that will enable you to remove people's names from the information you collect, and you should make provisions for the security of the key to that code.

5. How likely are you to ruffle someone's feathers by your attempts to measure attitudes?

Your answer to this question will determine how much attention you must pay to preparing people or reassuring them. It may even determine (as with the previous question) whether you decide to do without certain types of information.

This question deals with feelings rather than with ethics, although there is some overlap between the two.

Let us say, for example, that as part of the evaluation you decide to ask the parents of the students in the program for their opinions with such questions as these: "How satisfied were you with the variety of classroom activities in which your child participated?" "How satisfied were you that his or her assignments were at about the right level of difficulty?" You may find that the teachers in the program object to questions of this kind and will argue that parents are not in a position to make these judgments. Your explanation that the questionnaire is an *attitude* measure may not be sufficient to reassure them.

In business too, employees, clients, or customers may object to measuring attitudes if they are concerned that such an activity or its results may cause them a problem. For example, management may fear that a simple questionnaire about attitudes toward employee benefits may lead some employees to infer that changes WILL take place and to put undue pressure on management before it is ready to make a decision. Employees, on the other hand, may fear the professional consequences of expressing critical opinions or revealing certain feelings or traits on attitude surveys.

You may even find that some people will challenge all attitude measures by claiming that schools or companies have no business being concerned with attitudes or with trying to change attitudes. Such a point of view would confine the educational goals of the program to the realm of knowledge and skills, and similarly limit the evaluation.

These issues do not lend themselves to simple resolution. You may find it helpful to check with various key people, such as management, employees, teachers, parents, or administrators as you develop or select your measures. Assure them that you are evaluating a program, not people. Assure them that no persons will be identified or identifiable in any of your reports. Illustrate how the data will be used. "Test the water" as you go. It is far better to know beforehand whether people are likely to respond negatively to the measures you use, so that you can decide if obtaining the information is worth upsetting one group or another. Then if you decide to proceed, at least you can incur their displeasure knowingly. Unfortunately, evaluation of any kind carries with it judgmental connotations, no matter how gentle the approach of the evaluator.

In summary, this chapter has called your attention to five basic matters:

1. The need to decide on the relative importance of the attitude objectives within the total evaluation
2. The need to clarify and develop attitude objectives before attempting to make decisions about measurement techniques
3. The need to determine if the attitude measures for the program should focus on outcomes or processes
4. The need to attend to ethical or legal problems involved in the measurement of attitudes
5. The need to anticipate unfavorable reactions by various individual groups concerning the measurement of attitudes

NOTES

1. The term "audience," as used in the book, includes everyone to whom your evaluation report will be communicated, but *in particular* people who might use the information you provide to make decisions.

2. Some guidance in writing clear objectives is provided by *How to Focus an Evaluation*, Volume 2 of the *Program Evaluation Kit*, as well as by other sources listed at the end of the chapters. The book also describes procedures for determining priorities among objectives.

3. The advantages and disadvantages of various measurement procedures will be presented in Chapter 3 of this book.

Chapter 3
Selecting from Among Alternative Approaches to Collecting Attitude Information

Once you have clarified your attitude goals or objectives, you can begin to consider the types of information you will need and decide on the best approach for obtaining that information. This chapter is meant to help you consider the possibilities. It describes four general approaches and discusses their advantages and disadvantages.

If at this moment you already know what kinds of measurement instruments you need, you may wish to skip this chapter. If not, read on with the idea that by the time you reach the chapter's end, you will be in a position to make a decision at least about the kinds of instruments that will best serve your measurement needs.

Table 1 summarizes the four approaches discussed in this chapter. The first column lists the four types of measures. The second column lists the most appropriate circumstances for using each. The third column illustrates the kinds of questions the measures are likely to answer. The fourth column provides examples of the kinds of conclusions the measures can yield.

Approaches 1 and 2:
Self-Report and Reports of Others

Approach 1, self-report, includes all procedures by which a person can be asked to report on *his or her own* attitudes. The information can be provided *orally* through the use of interviews, surveys, or polls; it can be provided in *written* form through questionnaires, attitude rating scales, logs, journals, or diaries.

When you use self-report procedures, you assume that the people whose attitudes you are assessing have the self-awareness to recognize their own beliefs and feelings and the ability to articulate them. You also assume that they have no reason to lie about their attitudes.

Self-report procedures represent the most direct type of attitude assessment and should probably be employed unless you have reason to believe that the people whose attitudes you are investigating are unable or unwilling to provide the necessary information.

Even in situations where you have reason to doubt the accuracy of self-reports, you will probably be wise to collect them, double-checking them through another of the measurement approaches, such as reports of others. If, for example, you are evaluating an early childhood program that has as one of its major goals the creation of a pleasant and comfortable environment for children in the early grades, you could attempt to assess pupil comfort by questioning the children directly (self-report). But since the responses of young children are highly dependent upon the events of the moment (and therefore unreliable), you might turn to other sources for additional information—parents and teachers, for example.

Approach 2, reports of others, results in information that is based on *someone else's* assessment of a person's feelings, beliefs, or behavior. The reporter can either be someone who has had a relationship with the subject (e.g., a parent, teacher, co-worker, supervisor) or an independent observer who has had no previous contact with the subject. A common and credible attitude assessment method is to send trained observers who are not associated with the program into the classroom to report on the presence, absence, or frequency of certain kinds of behaviors.

Reports of others can be used in most of the same situations as self-report methods. Where the focus group is apt to be young or naive or biased, however, reports of others will likely be more credible. Reports of others will be, in addition, the desired method of attitude assessment in most situations where you want to report how people *behave*. This is because the report of people who saw the behavior is generally more credible than an after-the-fact self-report.

Reports of others range from recollections and informal observations of the subject to systematic observations based on a procedure using a specially trained reporter. There are many forms, both oral and written, in which reports of others are received, including anecdotal reports, responses to questionnaires, and tallies of the occurrence of specific behaviors as set forth in a checklist-type observation instrument.

One of your major concerns when you use procedures based on reports of others is the *objectivity* of the information you obtain. You must, of course, accept the fact that the information will be based on one person's observations of another person's behaviors—verbal and/or non-verbal. For the sake of producing credible results, you would like that information to be as unbiased as possible.

Another concern regarding reports of others has to do with the *completeness* of the information you receive. If the reporter has not had sufficient opportunity to observe a representative sample of behavior, the reported information could be misleading or completely irrelevant.

Although it is important to keep in mind the distinction between self-report and reports of others, both types of attitude measures usually make use of a common set of instrument types: interviews, surveys,

TABLE 1   Four Approaches For Evaluating the

	When is this approach most appropriate?
Approach 1: SELF-REPORT MEASURES (Members of Group X report directly about their own attitudes) • *interviews, surveys, polls* • *questionnaires and attitude rating scales* • *logs, journals, diaries*	When the people whose attitudes you are investigating • are able to understand the questions asked of them • have sufficient self-awareness to provide the necessary information • are likely to answer honestly and not deliberately falsify their responses
Approach 2: REPORTS OF OTHERS (Others report about the attitudes of members of Group X) • *interviews* • *questionnaires* • *logs, journals, reports* • *observation procedures*	When the people whose attitudes you are investigating are unable or unlikely to provide accurate information. When you want information about how people *behave* under certain circumstances. When you can assume that the reporter will be unbiased and will present objective information. When you can assume that the reporter has sufficient opportunity to observe a representative sample of behavior.
Approach 3: SOCIOMETRIC PROCEDURES (Members of Group X report about their attitudes toward one another) • *peer ratings* • *social choice techniques*	When you want a picture of the social patterns within a group
Approach 4: RECORDS • *counselor files* • *attendance records*	When you have access to records that provide information relevant to the attitudes in question and when these records are complete

Attitudes of Members of a Group or Groups

What kinds of questions can be answered by the measures?	Examples of the kinds of conclusions the measures can yield
(as a member of Group X) How do you feel about it? How strongly do you feel about it? ("It" may be any aspect of a program, focus of interest, or element of concern.) What do you believe about it? What are your reasons for believing as you do? What *should* you do? What have you done in the past? Which do you prefer to do?	Students in Program A have a greater tendency to attribute their school successes to their own efforts than do students in the control group. Staff in Program A are highly satisfied with the materials. Parents of children in Program A report greater satisfaction with the school and the progress of their children than do parents of children in Program B. Seventy-five percent of the employees in Program B have asked to continue in the program series.
(from your observations of Group X) What do they believe about it? How do they feel about it? How strongly do they feel about it? What do they do when confronted with it?	Parents of children in Program A report significant improvement in their children's work habits since the beginning of school. Teachers in Program A report that classroom friendship patterns indicate successful integration and acceptance of the bussed students. Observers report a significant difference in the number of helping behaviors exhibited by Program B staff as compared with control group staff.
(as a member of Group X) Who in your group fits this description? Whom would you choose in this situation? Who associates with whom?	The sociometric choices of students in Program A indicate that handicapped students are establishing friendships with students in the larger group. The sociometric choices of staff in Program B indicate that new immigrant workers are being accepted by the other staff.
What do past records indicate they (Group X) know about it? What inferences can be made from past records concerning their feelings about it? What do past records indicate they do when confronted with it?	Individuals in Program A tend to be absent less than those in Program B. There have been significantly fewer disciplinary referrals in Group X.

questionnaires, rating scales and written reports. Reports of others can, in addition, be collected through systematic observations. The following discussion will deal with the advantages and disadvantages of various kinds of instruments in the following categories:

- Interviews, surveys, and polls
- Questionnaires and attitude rating scales
- Logs, journals, diaries, and reports
- Observation procedures

Interviews, Surveys, and Polls:
Instruments Where the Response Is by Word-of-Mouth

An *interview* is a face-to-face meeting between two or more people in which the respondent answers questions posed by the interviewer. An interview may involve predetermined questions, but the interviewer is free to pursue interesting responses if he or she feels it useful. The interviewer records the respondent's answers in some way, usually by taking notes. The interviewer then develops a more complete summary after the meeting has been concluded.

The term *survey* refers to a highly structured interview that need not take place in a face-to-face situation. Frequently, surveys are conducted over the telephone. A *poll* is simply a headcount. The respondents are presented with a limited number of options: Are you for or against? Do you prefer Plan 1, 2, or 3?

Table 2 should help you determine which of these three might be most suitable in your situation.

TABLE 2
Instruments Requiring Word-of-Mouth Responses

	Type of Instrument		
	interview	survey	poll
amount of inter-viewing skill required	considerable	moderate	negligible
number of questions involved	many	moderate number	few
complexity of the response you wish to assess	complex	moderately complex	simple

Advantages of word-of-mouth procedures

Interviews, oral surveys, and polls have certain advantages that make them popular attitude evaluation tools:

- They can be used to obtain information from people who cannot read and from non-native speakers who might have difficulties with the wordings of questionnaires.
- The success rate in obtaining responses from the group you have selected will generally be higher than with questionnaires that are mailed or sent out.
- They are better than questionnaires for obtaining information that requires sequencing. A person answering a questionnaire cannot be prevented from reading ahead or changing answers. These problems do not exist with word-of-mouth procedures; questions must be answered in the sequence in which they are presented.

Interviews, in particular, permit flexibility in several ways:

- Interviewers can clarify the questions and ensure that the respondent understands them. They make judgments as to whether or not the respondent has sufficient knowledge to answer the questions. New lines of inquiry can be pursued based on the comments of the respondent.
- They allow for an estimation of the strength of an attitude. For example, Robert, when presented with a questionnaire that asks if he uses the employee cafeteria, can check the "no" box. But if, in

the interview situation, this question elicits a vehement "NO WAY!" you have an indication of the strength of Robert's feelings about the cafeteria.

- Interviews are an excellent first step into a complex issue. Probing interviews conducted with a representative sample of respondents can provide you with a sound basis upon which to develop a questionnaire for wider distribution.

Disadvantages of word-of-mouth procedures

Oral response procedures present two problems. *The first is that they are very time-consuming.* In some instances, you can overcome this time problem by selecting a small *sample* of the total group of people whose attitudes you are attempting to evaluate, and interviewing only those representative few.

The second problem has to do with the influence of the interviewer on the respondent. Questioning people orally in a formal situation can make them anxious. They become worried about why they are being questioned, what they are expected to say, and how their responses will be interpreted by the person asking the questions. These apprehensions are not completely absent in situations where people are asked to respond to questionnaires; but at least a questionnaire does not demand sitting there, being looked at. Nor can a questionnaire smile, frown, or raise an eyebrow, which an interviewer in some cases will do, in spite of honest efforts to avoid influencing the respondent. The interviewer is, in effect, the evaluation instrument. And the more likely it is that he or she will inhibit the respondents or cause them to modify their answers, the less you can depend on the information you receive.

You can reduce interviewer influence by selecting the interviewers carefully and seeing to it that they are trained in the basics of interviewing and are properly prepared for your situation. These and other interviewing concerns are discussed in Chapter 7, "Developing Your Own Measures: Interviews."

**Questionnaires and Attitude Rating Scales:
Instruments That Call for Written Responses**

Questionnaires and attitude rating scales are instruments that present information to a respondent in writing or through the use of pictures and then require a written response—a check, a circle, a word, a sentence, or several sentences.

Questionnaires are generally used in cases where the evaluator needs answers to a variety of questions. They are frequently designed so that each question can represent a discrete concern and can yield a score specific to that concern. They can also be designed, however, so that answers to several questions can be summed to yield a single score. For example, if a questionnaire contained a group of questions each of which asked how the respondent felt toward a particular aspect of school, then the number of favorable responses to these questions from each person could serve as a score for "overall attitude" toward the school.

Attitude rating scales are special kinds of questionnaires. They are developed according to strict procedures which ensure that several responses can be summed to yield a single score representing one attitude. The procedures for constructing attitude rating scales ensure consistency by discarding *erratic* items or questions. Erratic items are items that produce responses which are inconsistent with a person's responses to the other items. Constructing an attitude rating scale involves evaluating each question to determine the extent to which it serves to differentiate high from low scorers on the whole scale. Chapter 6 describes in detail how attitude rating scales are constructed.

Advantages and disadvantages of questionnaires and attitude rating scales

Questionnaires and attitude rating scales have certain advantages that make them popular attitude evaluation tools:

- They permit anonymity. If you arrange it so that the responses are given anonymously, you will increase your chances of receiving responses that genuinely represent a person's beliefs or feelings.
- They permit a person a considerable amount of time to think about his answers before responding.

- They can be given to many people simultaneously.
- They provide greater uniformity across measurement situations than do the interviews. Each person responds to exactly the same questions.

- In general, the data they provide can be more easily analyzed and interpreted than the data received from oral responses.
- They can be mailed as well as administered directly to a group of people, although you may find that you will have to work hard to get a good return rate.

A disadvantage of questionnaires is that they do not provide the flexibility of interviews. In an interview, as mentioned before, an idea or comment can be explored. This makes it possible to gauge how people are interpreting a question. If the questions you ask are interpreted differently from one respondent to another, the validity of the information you obtain is jeopardized. You have a better chance of spotting this kind of problem and correcting it in an interview situation.

Another disadvantage of questionnaires is that people are generally better able to express their views orally than in writing.

Attitude rating scales are useful if you can find one that covers the dimensions of the attitude you are interested in measuring. Keep in mind that, by themselves, score results from these instruments may not be convincing to your evaluation audience. You may find it necessary to supplement and corroborate score data with other kinds of information.

When to use which written-response form

If you have a variety of concerns, most of which can be covered by asking straightforward questions, consider the use of a questionnaire. Since you are not likely to find an existing questionnaire that will serve your particular needs, you must allow sufficient time to develop a set of questions and try them out.

If you are concerned with one particular attitude, and there is to be a heavy emphasis on attitude differences or attitude change, you would do well to use an existing and technically adequate attitude rating scale as one measure of the attitude in question.

Logs, Journals, Diaries, and Reports: Less Formal Written Accounts

Logs, journals, and *diaries* are descriptions of activities, experiences, and feelings written *during the course of the program.* Generally, they are running accounts consisting of many entries that are included either on a daily or weekly basis.

Participants in a program, for example, might be asked to keep a daily log in which they record any significant event of that day and their reactions to the event. These accounts could then be analyzed at the end of the program to determine the feelings of the participants toward various components of the program. In addition, the logs might reveal patterns of attitude change.

Whereas "diaries" usually are *self-report* instruments, it should be noted that logs and journals can be kept in order to report about *others.* A special education teacher, for instance, could keep a daily journal of his work with educationally handicapped students at a learning center. A repair service employee could keep a log of his or her encounters with customers while a new repair program is being implemented.

Written reports on the behavior or attitudes of others are generally done *in retrospect* and depend upon the reporter's powers of recall. The reporter may or may not have been informed beforehand (at the beginning of the program, for example) that he or she would be asked to prepare a report or fill out a questionnaire. Reporters of the attitudes of others are expected to know about the subject's attitudes or behavior because of some *past* or *ongoing* relationship with the subject (e.g., teachers preparing reports about their students; supervisors filling in questionnaires about their staff).

Advantages and disadvantages of logs, journals, and diaries

The advantage of these procedures is that they can provide a wealth of information about a person's experiences and feelings. The disadvantage lies in the problems involved in extracting, categorizing, and interpreting the information. This process requires a great deal of time and a certain amount of expertise.

You cannot use a procedure of this kind, of course, if you step onto the scene as the evaluator only at the end of the program, unless you find by some coincidence that such logs or journals already exist.

Advantages and disadvantages of written reports

One of the advantages of these procedures is that they can be designed to make minimal demands on the reporters. There is no special preparation required of the reporters, and the amount of time required can be controlled. People are willing to serve as reporters if the effort required of them is not too great. By consulting them, you are, furthermore, implying that their observations are important.

Another advantage is that someone who has had an ongoing relationship with another person is likely to have witnessed a wide range of behaviors. His or her report might be, for this reason, highly credible.

A disadvantage of reports is that they might demand considerable time to score and interpret. Formal and informal instruments often involve a trade-off—you either invest time in constructing the instrument or in processing the final data. In the case of questionnaires, for example, your job, preparing the instrument, may take a great deal of time, whereas scoring each questionnaire may take no more than a minute or two. If you use written reports, however, you may spend no time preparing an instrument, but you will likely be in for a lengthy scoring and interpretation process.

Another disadvantage of written reports is that the information they yield is frequently biased and incomplete. The bias is not intentional; it is just a natural outcome of the fact that people have mind sets that result in selective recall. Most people are not naturally good observers. *Unless they are instructed in advance to look for specific behaviors,* people remember only those behaviors which fit into their view of the world. Mr. Fry, for example, who has been in conflict with Sharon for the past six months, could very easily overlook small improvements in her behavior, especially since she is one of thirty people he has to deal with. He would most likely notice only Sharon's continued troublesome behavior once he became sensitized to it.

Observation Procedures

These procedures call for someone to devote all of his or her attention to the behavior of another *individual* or *group* within a natural setting and for a prescribed time period. In many cases, the instrument used to record what has been seen and heard in the observation provides detailed guidelines which include:

- The number of observations to take place
- The amount of time to be spent in any one observation period
- A detailed description of the behavior to be observed, telling how to decide whether, or to what degree, the behavior took place

- The specific method for recording the presence, absence, or frequency of the behavior, or its quality

For the purpose of measuring attitudes, observation procedures can help to identify changes in behavior over the course of an instructional program. They can help to detect differences in behavior between groups—for instance, between individuals in an experimental program and those in the control group. They can also help to determine the relationship between behaviors of students during the program and the eventual affective and cognitive outcomes of the program.

Forms for recording observations can be questionnaires, rating scales, or tally sheets. There are also less restrictive procedures for reporting what has been seen in the observation. An observer may be sent into a classroom, for example, without detailed guidelines and asked to write anecdotal accounts of significant events that occurred within the prescribed time period. Thus an observation report, in the sense discussed here, need be no more formal than the written accounts described in the last section. However, the observation report, unlike other written accounts, is an on-the-spot record by someone serving only in the capacity of observer.

Advantages and disadvantages of observation procedures

Whether using formal or informal procedures, an outside observer provides a different point of view than one who is involved in the activity observed. The advantage of using a formal observation procedure to measure the behavior of program participants lies in the increased credibility of this approach when a *pre-trained, disinterested* observer is used. Formal observation procedures direct the observer's attention to behaviors that might otherwise have been overlooked.

Formal observation procedures, of course, have their limitations. To begin with, they require time—time to develop an instrument if there isn't one available, time to train the observers, and time to collect a sufficient number of observations. You must ensure that what is seen and heard in any given observation period are fairly common occurrences in the program being evaluated, rather than extraordinary, atypical events. You must also ensure that different people using the observation instrument and viewing the same behavior will present the same findings.[1]

Another problem is the inevitable discomfort some people feel in having observers in their program. Then, too, the presence of the observer can to a degree alter what takes place.

Approach 3: Sociometric Procedures

Sociometric procedures are relatively simple tools for obtaining information about a group's social structure. These procedures elicit information from group members bearing on their attitudes toward one another. An item such as the following might be used with young children:

There is someone (in the class) who is nice to everybody and has lots of friends; guess who.

A popular type of item calls on individual members of a group to make reality-oriented social choices such as:

Name three people with whom you'd like to work in a committee.

The information obtained from sociometric procedures provides answers to such questions as these:

- Who are the group leaders?
- Who are the popular members of the group?
- What are the friendship patterns of the group?
- Which of its members does the group reject?

It is unlikely that you would need information of this kind for any group other than the people in the program, although sociometric methods might conceivably be used for evaluating a program aimed at changing patterns of interaction among nonparticipants as well.

Advantages

Sociometric procedures have the advantage of being easy to devise and use. The information they provide—a view of the peer-group world through the eyes of the participants—is probably obtainable in no other way. In conjunction with other methods, sociometric data can help evaluate the social outcomes of a program with respect to differences among the individuals—differences, for example, in ability levels, racial identification, or sex roles. They are particularly useful for evaluating programs that seek to integrate new people into a group, as when students with learning disabilities are placed in regular classrooms or when workers with a different cultural background or language are to be integrated in the work force.

Disadvantages

Sociometric instruments get group members to make subjective choices from among their peers, but they do not reveal the basis on which choices have been made. Primary grade children, for example, do not tend to make fine distinctions. If a child is chosen in one circumstance (work within a committee), it is likely that the same child will be chosen in all circumstances (sit next to, be on the same team with, etc.). Generally, the same few students are chosen by large numbers of the group, while less assertive students tend to be passed over. When you analyze the information, you find that you have a good picture of "who," but very little information about "why." As mentioned in Chapter 2, sociometric methods also raise certain ethical questions concerning the effect on the individual of the open knowledge of how popular they may or may not be within the group.

Approach 4: Records

Records are systematic accounts of regular occurrences. They consist of such things as:

- attendance and enrollment reports
- sign-in sheets
- library checkout records
- permission slips
- counselor files
- inventories
- staff reports
- personnel files

An ideal evaluation situation is one in which you are able to plan a record-keeping system that will function throughout the program. For example, if one of the affective goals of your program is to increase enjoyment of reading, you might consider frequency of use of the library as one possible measure. You could arrange *before the program gets underway:*

- To place a sign-in sheet at the library door, and/or
- To ask the people running the program (and the control group, if you are using one) to keep a record of requests to go to the library.

You should not be too hopeful of finding strong trends in such data; but if it is relatively easy to collect and report, you might as well check out the possibility.

Unfortunately, most evaluation situations are not ideal. In many instances, you will assume the role of evaluator after the program is well underway, and face either arranging for the recording of events during the remainder of the program, or gathering information from records that were kept for some other purposes (possibly program administration records).

It is frequently appropriate to examine *attendance records* if they are available. This will allow you to report the amount of time the students actually were in contact with the program. Whether or not you decide to use other existing records in your evaluation will depend on their availability and their value in providing you with the information you need.

If you do, on the other hand, have the opportunity to prepare a record-keeping system, you should work closely with the prospective record keepers to ensure that the process is not burdensome and, if at all possible, that the records be useful to them as well.

Advantages

Records that are kept independent of the program evaluation effort (e.g., attendance records, book circulation records) have the advantage of supplying data that was gathered without additional demands on people's time and energies. It is also true that people tend to view the information found in records as objective and therefore credible.

Disadvantages

A major disadvantage is that records are frequently incomplete, even those records that you have planned for well in advance. In the pressures of the day, people forget to sign in or record an event or keep track of all the relevant information. Another disadvantage is that the process of examining existing records can be time-consuming. When you have not had a part in deciding what kinds of records should be kept, you may find yourself spending hours sifting through reams of paper in an effort to cull and make sense of the relevant information. You can, however, relieve this burden by *sampling,* that is, by selecting a limited but representative portion of the records for consideration.

Still another problem is that there may be ethical or legal constraints involved in your use of certain kinds of records. Counselor or personnel files, for example, may not be open to inspection for ethical or legal reasons.

Selecting from Among the Approaches:
A Summary

Here is a brief summary to help you answer the question, "What kinds of instruments will best serve my measurement needs?"

IF the people whose attitudes you are investigating are able to understand the questions and have sufficient self-awareness to provide you with the necessary information,

and

IF they are likely to answer honestly and not deliberately falsify their responses ⎯⎯⎯⎯→ use SELF-REPORT PROCEDURES

IF the people whose attitudes you are investigating are unable or unlikely to provide you with accurate information,

or

IF you are reporting on how people *act* (how they behave under certain circumstances) ⎯⎯⎯→ use REPORTS OF OTHERS

IF you want a picture of the social patterns within a group ⎯⎯⎯⎯⎯⎯⎯⎯⎯→ use SOCIOMETRIC PROCEDURES

IF there are records that provide information with attitudinal implications, and if the records are complete ⎯⎯⎯⎯⎯⎯⎯→ use RECORDS

IF the attitude objectives are among the *major* objectives of the program ⎯⎯⎯⎯→ use A VARIETY OF THESE METHODS

NOTE

1. This critical attribute of an observation instrument is known as inter-rater reliability. It is discussed in Chapter 11.

Chapter 4
Finding an
Existing Measure

There are advantages to measuring attitudes using already existing measures. The obvious advantage is that you save time. Another advantage is that an existing measure will give you the benefit of other people's experience. The instrument will already have been tried out and should carry some reliability and validity data. You might even be able to find results from its past administrations to compare with your own.

If you examine the range of published attitude measures, you will find that the field is dominated by paper-and-pencil, self-report instruments. Although there is no shortage of observation schedules and rating scales, many of these were developed for purposes other than program evaluation and might require modification before you use them.

A good number of the various types of attitude measures are standardized and available on the commercial test market. "Standardized" here means that, regardless of whether norms (such as percentiles) are available with them, these instruments have a standard format for administration. They generally have been through a development phase during which they were validated on groups of subjects. When you purchase such measures, you will receive a technical manual that provides norms (if they are available) based on the scores of a tryout group, information on the validity and reliability of the instruments, and instructions for administering and scoring the results. Much of this information can be obtained without a commitment to buy if you write to the publishers requesting *specimen sets*. Most companies charge a small fee for specimen sets which usually consist of a sample copy of the instrument and an accompanying manual.

In addition to commercially available measures, you might be able to obtain "homemade" instruments developed by another school or district, or copyrighted instruments developed for research purposes at a university. Such measures may have been used extensively or only once or twice. They may or may not provide validity and reliability information. Their use may cost you nothing, or you may have to purchase copies from the author or pay for the right to reproduce your own copies. In some instances, you may be able to use an instrument in exchange for a promise to provide the developer with information on your findings. If there is a fee, it is likely to be less than you would pay for published, standardized measures.

The purpose of this chapter is to help you locate and choose among existing measures. The chapter is *not* meant to recommend a specific measure, but rather to help you:

- Determine what the attitude you want to measure is likely to be called in the literature or in catalogs of available tests
- Find reference books that list, describe, and/or evaluate existing measures
- Obtain and examine the measures that seem appropriate for your evaluation needs

Various Names for the Attitude You Want to Measure

Many attitude measures have names that are self-explanatory. Others do not. The trick is to find the labels that match the kinds of attitudes you wish to measure. These labels will be discussed in terms of five attitude categories that cover a broad range of questions often asked in program evaluation:

- attitudes toward self
- attitudes toward school and school-related concerns
- attitudes toward others
- attitudes toward vacations and general interests
- attitudes toward job satisfaction

If the type of instrument you are looking for is not mentioned in the next few pages, do not lose hope. The next section of this chapter will refer you to sources that should help you look further.

Category 1: Attitudes Toward Self

Many instruments, both for children and adults, attempt to measure some facet of this general attitude. You may find them referred to as measures of:

- self-esteem
- self-perception
- self-concept
- self-actualization
- personality integration
- ego strength
- self-confidence
- locus of control

The bulk of these instruments are paper-and-pencil, self-report measures that ask about everything from the way people feel about their looks to the degree of influence people feel they exert on the important events in their lives. Most of the terms listed are familiar or self-explanatory, but perhaps "locus of control" needs explaining.

Locus of control instruments attempt to measure the degree to which people feel that control of their successes and failures depends on themselves versus the degree to which they attribute their successes and failures to external factors. Developers of these instruments maintain that there is a strong correlation between high achievement motivation and the attribution of one's successes to one's own efforts.

The following are a few examples[1] of the kinds of paper-and-pencil, self-report measures that deal with Category 1—attitudes toward self.

Measure of Attitudes Toward Self	Grade Level Range	Publisher*
Piers-Harris Children's Self Concept Scale: a measure of attitudes towards one's physical attributes, intellectual and school status, behavior, popularity, happiness, and satisfaction	3-12	CRT
Tennessee Self Concept Scale: a measure of attitudes toward self in terms of physical, moral-ethical, personal, family, and social characteristics	7-12	CRT
Self-Esteem Inventory (Coopersmith): a measure of attitudes toward self in the school and home context; also includes behavior-rating form for teacher use	3-12	SEI
Intellectual Achievement Responsibility Questionnaire (Crandall): a measure of belief in one's control over academic and intellectual accomplishments and failures	3-12	Cr
Locus of Control Scale (Nowicki & Strickland): a measure of belief in one's control over personal accomplishments and failures both in and out of school	3-12	No

*Publishers' names and addresses are listed in Appendix A.

Category 2: Attitudes Toward School and School-Related Concerns

Educators have long suspected a relationship between attitudes and cognitive achievement. However, even if such a relationship did not exist, attitudes toward school would still be important indicators of children's happiness in a place where they are required to spend many hours per day. There are measures attempting to examine attitudes toward:

- specific school subjects
- schoolmates
- teachers
- the school environment
- learning as a process
- education in general

As you begin to examine some of these measures, you will notice that there is overlap among the four categories that are used here as organizers. For example, many measures that fall into Category 2 (attitudes toward school) could as easily be listed under Category 1 (attitudes toward self) since they contain sub-scales which investigate children's self-concepts in school situations. They could, in fact, even be listed under Category 3 (attitudes toward others) since they contain sub-scales which investigate children's attitudes toward teachers or peers. The reason for placing the following measures in Category 2 is that their questions or items are primarily *school* oriented.

The following are examples of paper-and-pencil, self-report measures that deal with Category 2—attitudes toward school and school-related concerns.

Measure of Attitudes Toward School	Grade Level Range	Publisher*
School Anxiety Questionnaire: a measure of the anxiety engendered by need to achieve, report cards, tests, recitation, failure	4-12	Du
Barclay Classroom Climate Inventory: a measure that provides resources for peer nominations and teacher judgments as well as assessment of student attitudes toward school in general	3- 6	ESD
School Morale Scale: a measure of attitudes toward school plant, instruction and instructional materials, community support and parent interest, schoolmates, teacher-student relations, school in general	4-12	Wr

Childhood Attitude Inventory for Problem Solving: a measure of beliefs about the nature of problem solving and of self-confidence in undertaking problem-solving activities	5- 9	Co
The Minnesota School Affect Assessment: a measure of attitudes toward academic subjects, school personnel, and other school conditions, with subscales that assess feelings of support, constraint, and self-worth	1-12	CED
Self-Concept as a Learner Scale: a measure of one's self-concept as a learner in the school context	4-12	Wa
Student Attitude Survey: a measure of attitudes toward the teacher, teaching processes, one's academic capabilities, and one's peer group	4-12	Mc
What I Like To Do: an instrument that assesses interest in various areas—play, academic subjects, art, occupations, reading	4- 7	SRA
Interest Inventory for Elementary Grades: an instrument that assesses the similarity of a child's interests to the interests of others of the same age and sex	3- 6	CPS

*Publishers' names and addresses are listed in Appendix A.

Classroom observation systems are another type of measure that should be mentioned in this category. Observation systems have been used extensively in research studies to examine the relationships between classroom practices and student attitudes and achievement. If your evaluation can be served by a systematized account of classroom behavior or classroom interaction patterns, you might wish to look at some of these systems. (The advantages of using systematic observation systems were discussed in the previous chapter.) There are many such observation systems. Here are the names of two:

Classroom Observation System	Grade Level Range	Publisher*
Flanders System: the focus of this system is on classroom affect; the observer records verbal exchanges between teacher and students	K-12	PAA

Spaulding Systems: the first of two systems codes motor and other nonverbal behavior of students related to affect; the second codes verbal and nonverbal behavior of teachers — K- 6 — EIP

---

*Publishers' names and addresses are listed in Appendix A.

Rating scales are another way to obtain information about student attitudes toward school. The ratings are made by teachers for each student based on estimates of classroom behavior typical for that student. The following are two of the many that exist:

Rating Scale	Grade Level Range	Publisher*
Devereux Elementary School Behavior Rating Scale: a measure of overt classroom behaviors which, according to teachers, either promote or interfere with learning	K- 6	DFP
Hahnemann High School Behavior Rating Scale: the same kind of measure as the one above, but appropriate for secondary school	7-12	HMC

*Publishers' names and addresses are listed in Appendix A.

Some instruments have been developed for those who are interested in measuring *teacher attitudes.* Here are the names of two paper-and-pencil, self-report instruments:

Measure of Teacher Attitudes	Publisher*
Minnesota Teacher Attitude Inventory: a measure of teacher attitudes toward children and toward how children learn	PC
Purdue Teacher Opinionaire: a measure of teacher morale as indicated by attitudes toward teacher salaries, work load, curriculum issues, school facilities and services, and teaching as a profession	PUBS

*Publishers' names and addresses are listed in Appendix A.

Category 3: Attitudes Toward Others

An assortment of instruments can be grouped under this category— measure of a person's:

- faith or trust in others
- acceptance of others
- concern for others
- strategies for dealing with others

- social insight
- attitudes toward group membership
- attitudes toward others of different races, cultures, or religions

In addition to the usual sources of measures, you might also investigate for this particular category the evaluation instruments that accompany various social studies curriculum projects. Sometimes these instruments are, in fact, measures of attitudes toward others. Although related to the curricular materials, some may be usable apart from the program.

An example of this is the *Intergroup Relations Curriculum,* an elementary school program produced by the Lincoln-Filene Center for Citizenship and Public Affairs at Tufts University in Medford, Massachusetts. This curriculum, which includes many learning activities and units, has as one of its objectives the reduction of stereotyped and prejudiced thinking and overt discrimination. Methods of evaluating a child's prejudice are described in the materials.

The following measures deal with Category 3—attitudes toward others.

Measure of Attitudes Toward Others	Grade Level Range	Publisher*
Cross-National Scales for Measuring Attitudes in Civic Education: a collection of measures of attitudes toward egalitarianism, citizenship, and civic responsibility; these measures were validated on children in the United States, Great Britain, and Germany and have been published by the ERIC Documents Reproduction Service. (The scales were developed by IEA which *officially endorses* their use only when users meet certain standards of administration, sampling, and data analysis. IEA stands for International Association for the Evaluation of Educational Assessment, an organization located in Stockholm, Sweden.)	5-12	ERIC

How to Assess the Moral Reasoning of Students (Nancy Porter & Nancy Taylor). "A teacher's guide to the use of Lawrence Kohlberg's Stage-Development Method," this booklet tells how to present five of Kohlberg's moral-problem stories, each followed by questions. Examples demonstrate how to score students' justifications according to Kohlberg's six stages of moral development (related to the stages of cognitive development described by Jean Piaget).	4-12	OI
Katz-Zalk Opinion Questionnaire: a measure of attitudes toward children of other races and children of the opposite sex; this measure requires the use of slides.	K- 6	Ka
Machiavellianism (adult version and child version): a measure of the degree to which a person feels that others are manipulable. This measure appears in the book *Studies in Machiavellianism* (Christie et al., 1970).	5-12	AP
Russell Sage Social Relations Test: an observation measure of the degree of cooperative group problem-solving behavior exhibited in two phases— planning and construction; the group is required to build three structures of varying complexity; for children, the building materials are interlocking plastic blocks.	4-12	ETS

*Publishers' names and addresses are listed in Appendix A.

Category 4: Attitudes Toward Vocations and General Interests

This category refers to preferences that might lead to a choice of life work and related interests.

The following are a few of the many available:

Measure of Attitudes Toward Vocations and Allied Interests	Grade Level Range	Publisher*
Minnesota Vocational Interest Inventory: an instrument that assesses interests and compares them with the interests of people in various occupations, with an	10-12	PC

emphasis on "blue-collar" and
service occupations

Strong-Campbell Interest Inventory: an instrument that assesses interests and compares them with the interests of people in various occupations, with an emphasis on professional and business occupations	10-12	SUP
Kuder Occupational Interest Survey: an instrument that yields a profile of interest scores in several categories, including mechanical, computational, and artistic interests	7-12	SRA
Career Maturity Inventory: an instrument that provides two scales, one an assessment of attitudes toward work and the other an assessment of competence in a work situation	7-12	CTB
Work Values Inventory: an instrument that assesses work values in terms of the values deemed important to a person's satisfaction in various occupations	7-12	HM

*Publishers' names and addresses are listed in Appendix A.

Category 5: Attitudes Toward Job Satisfaction

For more than fifty years there have been studies and reports on job satisfaction using over one hundred different types of attitude, morale, climate, and related types of questionnaires. Many of these studies have related job satisfaction to productivity, turnover, absenteeism, and so forth. During this time certain items and categories have been consistently used. These include:

- character and quality of supervision
- physical and general working conditions
- communications
- opportunities for personal growth and advancement
- status and recognition
- pay and benefits
- nonfinancial rewards

Several organizations maintain extensive files of items used across the wide variety of situations in which job satisfaction data can be collected. These organizations include the Industrial Relations Center of the University of

Minnesota, the Industrial Relations Center of the University of Chicago, the Survey Research Center at the University of Michigan, and Science Research Associates in Chicago. In many cases it is possible to have normative information on a national basis or on an industrywide basis for areas such as pay, benefits, communications, and supervisory-employee interpersonal relations.

The following measures are a sample of those dealing with attitudes toward job satisfaction.

Measure of Attitudes Related to Job Satisfaction	Grade Level Range	Publisher*
SRA Attitude Survey: Covers employee attitude toward 15 areas of work environment; for group measurement only. Available in French, Spanish, and Portuguese versions. Has several optional supplements.	Adult	SRA
Minnesota Satisfaction Questionnaire: Covers job satisfaction in business and industry, e.g., ability utilization, authority, company policy and practices, responsibility, status, supervision. Short and long forms available.	Adult	VPR
Management Burnout Scale: Self-administered multiple-item test for groups or individuals assesses burnout or work stress.	Adult	LHP
Stress Evaluation Inventory: Multiple-choice inventory evaluates stress that individuals are experiencing in their lives and identifies probable sources. Used in conjunction with stress management programs in business, health care, education, government, and private counseling settings.	Adult	IPAT

*Publishers' names and addresses are listed in Appendix A.

Reference Books That List, Describe, or Evaluate Existing Measures

This section briefly describes several bibliographical sources that could be of use in your search for an existing measure. These compendia offer extensive lists of available tests. They name many more than could possibly have been listed in this booklet.

Boyer, E. G., Simon, A., & Karafin, G. R. (Eds.). (1973). *Measures of maturation.* Philadelphia: Research for Better Schools, Humanizing Learning Program.

This is a three-volume anthology of 73 early childhood observation systems. Most of these systems were developed for research purposes, but some can be used for program evaluation.

The 73 systems are classified according to:

- The kinds of behavior that can be observed (individual actions and social contacts of various types)
- The attributes of the physical environment
- The nature and uses of the data and the manner in which it is collected
- The appropriate age range and other characteristics of those observed

Each system is described in detail.

Comrey, A. L., Backer, T. E., & Glaser, E. M. (1973). *A sourcebook for mental health measures.* Los Angeles: Human Interaction Research Institute.

This is a volume of approximately 1100 abstracts of lesser-known questionnaires, observation instruments, inventories, tests, and other measures. These measures are listed according to categories (e.g., Educational Adjustment/Primary and Elementary Schools, Educational Adjustment/ Secondary Schools, Racial Attitudes, Student Attitudes, Teacher Attitudes, and Teacher Evaluation). Each abstract identifies the measure, briefly describes it and tells how to obtain a copy.

Johnson, O. G., & Bommarito, J. W. (1971). *Tests and measurement in child development: A handbook.* San Francisco: Jossey-Bass.

This book lists and describes non-commercial measures that appeared in the literature—in this case, between the years 1956 and 1965.

According to the authors, the criteria for inclusion of a measure were:

- That it be suitable for children that fall within the age range of birth to 12 years old
- That it be available to other professionals
- That it come with sufficient information on administration and scoring procedures to make it usable

The measures include self-report and observation instruments, rating scales, structured interviews, sociometric measures, and projective personality tests. They are categorized (e.g., self-concept, perceptions of environment, social behaviors) and briefly described. Information for obtaining the measures is also provided.

Knapp, J. (1972). *An omnibus of measures related to school based attitudes.* Princeton, NJ: Educational Testing Service, Center for Statewide Educational Assessment.

This is a bibliography of 16 paper-and-pencil, self-report inventories. For each instrument there is a description of its contents, the subjects with whom the instrument has been used, the response mode, and the scoring procedures. There are also comments on the general usefulness of the instrument.

Mitchell, J. V. (Ed.). (1985). *The mental measurements yearbook.* Lincoln, NB: The University of Nebraska Press.

The Mental Measurements Yearbook provides a detailed description of each test and includes information on its norms, the time needed for administration, the number of forms available, and the cost. Most important, *MMY* provides reviews and evaluations written by two or more specialists in appropriate fields. For those who wish to investigate a particular test in greater depth, a bibliography of journal articles follows the reviews.

Mitchell, J. V. (Ed.). (1983). *Tests in print.* Lincoln, NB: The University of Nebraska Press.

Tests in Print provides a comprehensive list of all manner of standardized paper-and-pencil tests printed in English—tests of achievement, aptitudes, intelligence, and attitudes, with information about the group for whom the test is intended, when the test was developed, what the test is for, and, frequently, references to reviews of the test in *The Mental Measurements Yearbook.*

These two collections—*The Mental Measurements Yearbook* and *Tests in Print* (formerly by Buros)—are highly regarded references used extensively by people in psychology, education, and business. You are likely to find them in the reference section of any university or college library.

Robinson, J. P., & Shaver, P. R. (1973). *Measures of social psychological attitudes.* Ann Arbor, MI: Survey Research Center, Institute for Social Research, University of Michigan.

In this text the authors discuss and evaluate a variety of paper-and-pencil attitude instruments falling into several categories (e.g., values, self-esteem and related constructs, attitudes toward others).

One chapter is devoted to each category. Each chapter introduction discusses the types of instruments found in the category and the problems that are associated with each type. The body of the chapter reproduces part or all of each instrument and discusses each in detail, presenting information on the instrument's purpose, format, technical qualities, norm group, strengths and weaknesses, etc.

The instruments in each chapter are listed in an order which roughly reflects the authors' evaluations of them—the first ones listed being the more highly recommended.

Rosen, P. (Ed.). (1973, February). *Attitudes toward school and school adjustment, grades 4-6*. Princeton, NJ: Educational Testing Service.

This is a bibliography listing 31 available measures of attitudes toward school and school adjustment. Included among these are self-report, paper-and-pencil instruments, and observation instruments. Each of the references is briefly annotated.

Rosen, P. (Ed.). (1973). *Measures of self-concept*. Princeton, NJ: Educational Testing Service.

This is another bibliography similar to the one previously mentioned. In it are listed a variety of instruments including behavior rating scales, observation instruments, self-report and projective measures.

Rosen, P. (1973). *Self-concept measures: Head start test collection*. Princeton, NJ: Educational Testing Service.

This bibliography lists 44 measures published between 1963 and 1972. They pertain to the assessment of self-concept and are appropriate for use with children ranging in age from pre-school through third grade. Included are self-report, projective, and observation instruments. There is also a list of publishers' names and addresses to facilitate sending for specimen sets.

Simon, A., & Boyer, E. G. (1973). *Mirrors for behavior: An anthology of classroom observation instruments*. Philadelphia: Research for Better Schools. Center for the Study of Teaching.

This collection provides abstracts of 99 classroom observation systems. Each abstract contains information on the subjects of the observation, the setting, the methods of collecting the data, the type of behavior that is recorded, and the ways in which the data can be used. In addition, an extensive bibliography directs the reader to further information on these systems and how they have been used by others.

An earlier edition of this work (1967) provides detailed descriptions of twenty-six of these systems.

Sweetland, R. C., & Keyser, D. J. (Eds.). (1983, 1984). *Tests* and *Tests Supplement.* Kansas City: Test Corporation of America.
This comprehensive resource for assessments in psychology, education and business provides title, purpose, description, cost, publisher and other information on over 3000 tests.

Obtaining and Examining Attitude Measures

You should find out all you can about the development, administration procedures, and previous uses of any instrument you are considering. For commercially published tests, you can probably obtain specimen sets and manuals. For measures which are in development or "homemade," such information may or may not be available.

The following sample letters might be of help to you in sending for specimen sets of published tests or requesting relevant information about those that are not published.

Try to send your requests for information well before you will need the tests—perhaps two to three months in advance.

When the sample measures arrive, you will want to look them over with a critical eye. The six questions in the following section should be asked about any measure you are considering. If you are able to find an evaluation of a particular measure in the literature (e.g., in the books by Hoepfner, Miller, or Robinson, described earlier in this chapter), you have a good start in answering them. If not, you must depend on the information provided by the developers of the instrument and a close examination of the items or procedures included in the instrument. Perhaps someone in your school system or business or at a nearby college will be able to help you select from the attitude measures you are considering.

Six Questions

Before using any instrument, make sure you are satisfied with the answers to the following questions:[2]

1. *Does the measure seem to be doing what it says it does?* To help you answer this, think about how a skeptic would criticize the instrument by reinterpreting a score at either extreme. For example, suppose that an instrument purporting to determine a young child's comfort in the school environment presents the child with sets of pictures depicting these activities, one of which is school related. The non-school related activities include such things as staying at home, going to the zoo, watching television, and so forth. The child is asked to circle the one he

Example. Letter requesting specimen set

Mountain Unified School District · Board of Education · 11 North Pine Rd. · Mountain, California 96177

Gentlemen:

Your instrument, (*The X Inventory*) has come to our attention as one that might be useful to us in evaluating the affective goals of our (*new fourth grade reading program*).

Unless your specimen sets cost more than ($), would you please send us one and bill us. We would also appreciate any additional information that might help us determine whether this instrument suits our needs.

Thank you for your prompt attention to this matter.

Sincerely,

Name, Title, and/or
School Affiliation

likes best. Now suppose the child scores low, that is, consistently chooses non-school activities. The skeptic might say that the child's consistent preference for non-school related activities does not necessarily indicate discomfort or unhappiness in school. That child might just happen to like other activities better.

Turn yourself into a skeptic through this brief exercise: Imagine that you are committed to a particular program which you feel is having positive effects. The evaluation instrument under consideration has been given and has shown that the program is producing no effect—or even negative effects. How would you explain away this unwanted

Example. Letter requesting a measure and additional information

---

Copper Falls County School System
1400 Minocqua Drive
Ironwood, Michigan 49938
(412) 772-0047

Gentlemen:

Your instrument, (*The X Inventory*), has come to
our attention as one that might be useful to us in
evaluating the affective goals of our (*new eighth-
grade social studies program*).

Would you please send us a copy to examine and
any validation and reliability information that will
help us determine whether (*The X Inventory*) meets our
needs. We are also interested in the names and
addresses of others who have used it for purposes
similar to ours. (*Our target population is a group
of eighth graders of Indian-American ancestry.*)

Finally, if we decide to use (*The X Inventory*),
we will need information relevant to obtaining and
scoring (*80*) copies.

Thank you for your prompt attention to this
matter.

Sincerely,

Name, Title, and or
School Affiliation

---

result? In other words, how would you attack the instrument's credibility? If such an attack could be mounted with plenty of ammunition—for example, if you could make a case that many of the items are silly and misleading—then the instrument is not very credible and might not be valid.

2. *How close a fit is there between the objectives of the measure and your program objectives?* Let us say, for example, that you are examining a self-esteem instrument. In your examination you discover only one item that relates to pride of accomplishment. Yet this dimension of

self-esteem is heavily emphasized in your program goals. If you decide to purchase the instrument, you will have to tap this dimension through the use of some other measure. You should look for the measure that reflects *your* program objectives most accurately; in this case, one that measures all the components of self-esteem that *you* want to measure. Otherwise, you might find yourself attempting to evaluate the program using either irrelevant or insufficient data.

3. *Is there information on the reliability of the measure, and is this information persuasive?* Reliability information, as discussed in Chapter 11, can tell you how stable a measurement you are making. As you read about a particular instrument, you will notice that the degree to which it yields consistent results is expressed as a "reliability coefficient" which is a decimal. It is helpful to think of this decimal as representing the correlation between two administrations of the measure without intervening influences (e.g., instruction, acquisition of new information, change of attitudes). Thus a reliability of 1.00 would indicate a perfect correlation: two administrations of the measure without intervention yield exactly the same results. A reliability of zero would mean that the measure is totally useless.

In general, a measure used to make decisions about an *individual* should have a reliability of at least .90. One for making decisions about different *groups* or *programs* may be useful even if its reliability is as low as .50. Quite often an attitude instrument will not be accompanied by reliability estimates. In this case you will have to make an assessment of the instrument's credibility based on your own critical judgment.

4. *Does the measure seem appropriate for the age and ability level of the group whose attitudes you are measuring?* The instrument may be wrong for the group you have in mind for any one of several reasons: vocabulary, formatting, tone, etc. People have developed, for example, group measures for first graders with answer sheets requiring the children to record their responses on a complex matrix. Knowing that young children's perceptual skills are not up to this task, one can be sure that there will be many errors on such a measure simply because children will lose their places on the answer sheets. Older students or adults, on the other hand, given an attitude measure that is "below them" in language and format, will find it silly. Your data will be distorted accordingly.

5. *Can you anticipate any problems that might arise from the use of the measure?* Before you decide upon an instrument, try to see it through the eyes of those who will be involved—teachers, parents, administrators, students, employees, management, clients, or customers. If the measure is likely to offend one group or another, then you must bal-

ance the potential discomfort against the usefulness of the measure. *Information that is not required for appropriate program decisions is not worth collecting*—especially if its collection causes resentment.

6. *Do you have the wherewithal to do what has to be done to use the instrument?* This is the issue of practicality. For example, an observation schedule using an elaborate coding system will provide data that have to be decoded before they can be analyzed. Decoding is an extra step which will require extensive clerical assistance.

Before you decide on a measure, think of the step-by-step procedures involved in its use so that you can determine if the available time, money, and staff are adequate for the task.

Notes

1. Various factors were considered in choosing instruments to serve as examples in this chapter. Some were selected because they are frequently mentioned in the education literature; others, because their developers responded to requests for information; still others, because they seem to be the only instruments available for the measurement of a particular constellation of attitudes. Please note that no instrument *evaluation* was conducted for this book. Mention of specific instruments, therefore, should not be taken as an endorsement. To obtain more complete information, you should consult the resources mentioned later in this chapter where you might find the names of other available measures.

2. Some of these questions are directly related to validity and reliability concerns. For a more extensive discussion of these topics, see Chapter 11.

Chapter 5
Developing Your Own Measures: Questionnaires

This chapter provides suggestions to help you develop an effective questionnaire. These suggestions are organized according to the following eight steps:

1. Identify the program objectives for which the questionnaire is being prepared; determine what specific information you hope to obtain from the questionnaire.
2. Choose a response format.
3. Identify the frame of reference of the respondents.
4. Write the questions.
5. Prepare a data summary sheet.
6. Critique the questions; try them out and revise them.
7. Assemble the questionnaire.
8. Administer the questionnaire.

Step 1. Identify the program objectives for which the questionnaire is being prepared; determine what specific information you hope to obtain from the questionnaire.

In the following example, the evaluator has made a *list of the information* she will need to assess the attainment of a very general program goal. Having decided that she will use *two* self-report questionnaires to elicit the necessary information—one for students and one for teaching staff—she has consulted with the program planners and determined that for the students the relevant aspects of the program are the materials and the activities. For the staff, the relevant aspects of the program are the materials, the activities, and the administrative procedures.

Example

Program objective: The students and museum teaching staff will have positive attitudes toward the museum's art appreciation program for adults.

Information to be obtained from the questionnaire given to the students:

1. How did the students respond to the materials?
   a. Which ones did they use?
   b. Which ones did they like? Dislike? Why?

2. What were their reactions to the small group activities?
   a. Did they participate? What specific tasks did they perform?
   b. Did they feel they had opportunities to lead their group?
   c. Did they feel their ideas were accepted and valued by the others in their group?
   d. Did they feel they made a contribution?
   e. Did they feel pride in their group's accomplishments?
   f. Did they enjoy the activities? Why or why not?

Information to be obtained from the questionnaire given to the teaching staff:

1. How did the staff respond to the materials?
   a. Which ones did they use?
   b. Which ones did they like? Dislike? Why?

2. Did they find the small group activities a successful teaching tool?
   a. Did they feel the students profited from the activities? Enjoy them?
   b. How difficult was it to organize and carry out the small group activities?

3. Did they feel the program functioned smoothly?
   a. Did they get their materials on time? In sufficient quantities?
   b. Did they feel they received sufficient instruction in the use of the materials and procedures?

What if you find you are not able to determine the specific information you are seeking? Perhaps you want to know what people like or dislike about something, but you have no further categorization of the situation to help you write questions. In that case, you should conduct a few informal interviews before composing the questionnaire. This practice will serve as protection against constructing a questionnaire that yields inadequate information.

Example. At Edison Elementary School there has been widespread dissatisfaction with the after-school recreation program. You have been asked to conduct an evaluation of the program and to make suggestions for its improvement. You are thinking of using one or more questionnaires, but you are not certain about the specific areas of concern. You interview three teachers and three students and discover the following feelings and attitudes:

Teacher 1: Kids nowadays have no respect for property. They litter the yard and abuse the equipment and facilities. Kids who do this shouldn't be allowed to play on the yard after school.

Teacher 2: The play yard is so ugly and poorly equipped that the kids don't use it very much. They'd rather play on the street. We should plant some trees and flowers and get some new equipment—make it a pleasant place so that kids will want to use it.

Teacher 3: What we need is someone to organize the games and direct the play. And I don't think it's fair to ask us to volunteer to supervise after school. We should pay someone to do it.

Student 1: I never play there. Some adult is always telling you what to do. It's like school work, not play.

Student 2: I never play there. The big kids pick on you and there's no one around to make them stop.

Student 3: What's the use of playing there? The same group of kids is always hogging the balls and you always have to wait in line to use the bars and rings.

These interviews give evidence that there is indeed dissatisfaction. And though the reasons for it are diverse and somewhat contradictory, they tend to focus on physical facilities and lack of supervision. You can now formulate your questions around these topics. The additional time you spent interviewing may have saved you from developing an instrument whose inadequacies came to light only after it was administered at the loss of much time and energy.

Step 2. Choose a response format.

Will the questionnaire be composed of *closed* response questions, *open* response questions, or a combination of the two? A questionnaire that calls for closed responses provides alternative answers for each question or item, and the respondent is asked to choose from among these answers.

Example from a questionnaire for students

Here is a list of materials that were part of the art appreciation program:

	Did you use them?		If yes, were they helpful?			Were they fun to use?		
	yes	no	yes	no	uncer-tain	yes	so-so	no
workbooks	□	□	□	□	□	□	□	□
slides	□	□	□	□	□	□	□	□
posters	□	□	□	□	□	□	□	□
text	□	□	□	□	□	□	□	□
artist's tools & materials	□	□	□	□	□	□	□	□

A questionnaire that calls for open responses requires that the respondents write out the answers in their own words.[1]

Example from a questionnaire for students

Give us your opinions on the following materials that were part of the sixth-grade language arts program. How did you like them? Were they easy or hard to use? Were they helpful? Were they fun to work with?

1. Workbooks _____
   _____
   _____

2. Word game _____
   _____
   _____

3. Science-fiction books _____
   _____

Your decision depends on several factors:

- The number of respondents
- The amount and type of information you need
- The amount of time you have to process and interpret the information
- The extent to which you are able to anticipate the range of possible answers

If you have more than 20 or 30 respondents, you will almost certainly want to use a closed-response format. The closed-response format enables you to produce summaries of the results quickly and accurately, whereas reading numerous lengthy paragraph responses and then summarizing them is a very time-consuming procedure.

Open-response formats do have certain advantages:

1. They permit the ventilation of feelings. People can express their exact opinion in an open-ended response whereas if asked to simply check items they may feel that they have been forced into responses that do not exactly match their attitudes.
2. Open-ended questions may produce responses which draw the evaluator's attention to a situation or outcome that was unanticipated when constructing the questionnaire.
3. Open-ended questions do not limit the range of possible answers as do closed-response questions. For example, if you want to know about people's most salient impression of a program, an open question asking for impressions is better than a checklist of possible responses.

Most questionnaires include one or two open-ended items, therefore, to permit some ventilation of feelings, to uncover unanticipated outcomes, and to obtain some unprompted responses. It is generally best, however, to use closed-response formats for the major portion.

Using a format that calls for both open and closed responses is a way of treading the middle ground between a restrictive questionnaire and one which is wide open. A major advantage of this kind of questionnaire is that you are assured of having a score for the closed section of the questionnaire, and you have the option of deciding later if there is time to score the open section. Here are two examples of "mixed" questionnaires for teachers or program managers:

Examples

Help us measure the success of the program. Check one box for each of the numbered categories. Please explain "poor" ratings. If you have ideas as to how program materials or administration could have been improved, please share them with us.

Program Materials	excel-lent	good	fair	poor	unable to judge
1) the availability of the materials	☐	☐	☐	☐	☐
2) the quality of the materials (the quality of their content)	☐	☐	☐	☐	☐
3) the durability of the materials	☐	☐	☐	☐	☐
4) the quantity of materials available	☐	☐	☐	☐	☐
5) the suitability of the material for your students	☐	☐	☐	☐	☐
Administration of Program					
6) the procedures by which you were introduced to the program and the materials	☐	☐	☐	☐	☐
7) the procedure by which you obtained materials	☐	☐	☐	☐	☐
8) the procedure by which the facilities were made available	☐	☐	☐	☐	☐

Reasons for poor rating: Suggestions for improvement in problem areas:

_____   _____
_____   _____
_____   _____

Please rate the following materials. If you check the "poor" category, please give us your reasons for doing so.

	excel-lent	good	fair	poor	unable to judge
1) workbooks					
2) filmstrips					
3) biographies					
4) games					

Reasons for "poor" ratings: _____

_____
_____

Note that in many cases it is necessary to have a "no answer" option (e.g., the "unable to judge" columns in the previous examples). If a teacher *did not* use the filmstrips, for example, he would need a suitable response option. Without it, he might decide to leave a blank, and blanks are difficult for you to interpret: Did the respondent forget to answer? Refuse to answer? In addition, people become irritated when faced with forced-choice questions that do not provide them with appropriate response options.

Questions for Young Children

Although a questionnaire is not the best way to obtain information about the attitudes of young children, it can be used if you are so short of time that you must use a group-administered measure. You will have to be willing, however, to accept the results of such a measure knowing that paper-and-pencil, self-report measures for young children have a rather low level of reliability.

The major problems hindering attitude assessment in children are short attention span and the child's inability to understand questions and keep his place. To help children understand what is expected of them, response options are sometimes presented in picture form rather than in words. The child is then asked to select the picture that she *likes best* or that is *most like* her. This four-face response is a typical example:

Regardless of whether the questions consist of words or pictures, each item must be very carefully explained (or read) to the children, and the instructions for responding must be repeated over and over. If you decide to administer a questionnaire to a large group of young children, you should probably have assistants who can circulate among the children to make sure the questions are being understood and that the children are marking their answers in the appropriate places.

One method for helping children *keep their places* is to provide pictures at the side of each question and to separate questions with bold lines as in the following example:

	I listen to my teacher	YES	SOMETIMES	NO
	I bother others by talking too much	YES	SOMETIMES	NO
	I ask the teacher for help when I need it	YES	SOMETIMES	NO

There should also be several *practice items* to provide an opportunity for the children to learn how to respond before beginning the questionnaire. Even in the case of instruments administered to groups of adults, sample items are a good way to make sure that the respondents understand what they are asked to do.

Try to circumvent attention span problems by keeping the questionnaire short, perhaps even administering it in several brief sessions. Or you might try making the administration into a game against the clock: "Another group finished this in 15 minutes. Let's see if we can do better than that."

A useful procedure is to tape the questions and administer the instrument by playing the tape. This standardizes the administration, eliminates the need for reading instructions, and usually causes the respondents to attend closely. One clever evaluator kept the attention of very young children by introducing, on tape, a horse named Mary and a bull named Max. Horse and bull pictures appeared before alternate questions on the response form, and corresponding questions were asked by the appropriate male or female voice.

Four Types of Closed-Question Formats

There are several kinds of question formats that can be used in con-structing closed-response questionnaires. The following section provides examples, explanations, and suggestions for constructing four of the more commonly used formats: checklists, two-way questions, multiple-choice questions, and ranking scales.

Checklists. A checklist is a relatively simple tool. It is generally used to verify the presence or absence of some phenomenon, and may be intro-duced by a question, such as:

- Which of these materials did you use?
- Which of these activities did you engage in?
- Which of these are part of the program?

You might, for example, wish to use a checklist to determine whether or not someone knows what the program offers or what it involves, before you ask whether or not the person likes it.

The major criterion for a good checklist is that it contain all relevant options. Providing an "other" option for respondents to fill in at the end of a checklist sometimes helps to ensure that nothing is left out.

Example

Check as many boxes as necessary. These are the things
I have done this past semester in the after-school
recreation program:

Games:

☐ chess   ☐ bridge

☐ dominos   ☐ puzzles

☐ checkers   ☐ other (please name)_____
                             _____

Crafts:

☐ working with clay   ☐ craft projects

☐ doing macramé   ☐ building with blocks

☐ painting pictures   ☐ other (please name)_____
                             _____

Sports:

☐ handball   ☐ riding bikes

☐ baseball   ☐ riding bigwheels

☐ playing on bars   ☐ playing with stilts

☐ playing on rings   ☐ other (please name)_____

☐ having races   _____

Two-way questions. The two-way question presents two dichotomous alternatives—yes/no, approve/disapprove, for/against, true/false, good/bad, favor/oppose—although a third "no opinion" alternative is sometimes offered. The two-way question format can reduce issues to their simplest terms and force a choice.

```
Will you sign up to teach in this program
next semester?
```

☐ yes   ☐ no

It makes the tabulation of responses an easy task.

Your major concern in using this format is that *the two alternatives must present a realistic choice.* The following item, for instance, is poorly stated using a two-way format:

```
People who are in Program A are making more pro-
gress than people in Program B.
```

☐ agree   ☐ disagree

It would be better stated using a multiple-choice format, since the choice is not really a dichotomous one:

```
In comparison to people in Program B, the people
in Program A are:
```

☐ making more progress

☐ making less progress

☐ making about the same amount of progress

☐ I'm not able to make a judgment at this time

For the sake of clarity and fairness, a two-way question should state both alternatives. A question such as, "Do you think Program X should be repeated next semester?" might elicit a "no" response from a person who feels that the program needs modification. When confronted with a statement of both alternatives, "Do you think the Program X should be repeated next semester, or do you think it should be dropped?" the same respondent may elect to continue the program, deciding that a faulty program is better than no program at all. Providing both decision alternatives will save you from being accused at some future time of having misled the respondents.

The category of two-way questions also includes those which allow a noncommital response as a third option for the respondent who cannot reach a decision or who has no basis on which to make a choice.

Example

	agree	dis-agree	uncer-tain
1) Parents should have a voice in student placement.			
2) Teachers should be the ones to make the final decisions as to where their students should be placed next semester.			
3) Student placement procedures at our school are haphazard.			

Multiple-choice questions. Multiple-choice questions are useful when there are several possible responses, and you want to ensure that the respondent is aware of all the possibilities.

```
Of all the materials that came with the new program,
the set I used most was:
[ ] the slides          [ ] the textbooks
[ ] the workbooks       [ ] I didn't use any of
[ ] the wall charts         the materials
```

They are also useful for determining gradations of attitudes:

Examples

How informative were the following aspects of the
"Back-to-School" night? Please check one box for each
line (1-4) below.

	very informative	informative	moderately informative	marginally informative	not at all informative
1) conference with teachers					
2) display of class project					
3) pamphlets describing the math program					
4) introduction given by principal					

How do you feel about the new program?

☐ It's fine the way
   it is.

☐ It needs some modifi-
   cation.

☐ It needs extensive
   modification.

☐ It's not worth saving.

☐ Other (explain)_____
_____
_____

When constructing multiple-choice questions, you must make sure that
the alternatives are properly balanced and that each question explores only
one idea.

The following example is *unbalanced*. It attempts too much by trying
to find out (a) whether people prefer the old or new program, and (b) the
degree to which people feel the new program should be changed. The
result is that the alternatives are loaded in favor of the new program.

Example of an unbalanced multiple-choice question

How do you think the new program compares with the old
program?

☐ The new program is better and needs little or no
   modification.

☐ The new program is better, but it needs some modification.

☐ The new program is better, but it needs extensive modification.

☐ The new program is no better or worse than the old program.

☐ The new program is not as good as the old program.

You should also make sure that the alternatives represent *mutually exclusive categories*—that there is no overlap from one alternative to another. In the following example, alternatives 2 and 3 clearly overlap. Alternative 4 is confusing and could be interpreted as overlapping with 2, 3, or 5.

Example of overlapping multiple-choice alternatives

Which one of these would you consider the most important aspect of an early childhood program?

☐ 1) teaching children to read

☐ 2) teaching children to work and play well with one another

☐ 3) teaching children how to make and keep friends

☐ 4) helping children feel comfortable in the school environment

☐ 5) helping children to develop confidence in their ability to learn

Eliminating 3 and 4 would improve this question.

Ranking scales. This format gives you an indication of how a person ranks a number of things in relation to one another. It is a useful format when there are a limited number of things you would like to have ranked (probably not more than five). To avoid confusion in tabulating responses to this kind of question, you should specify that tie-rankings are not allowed.

Example

How do you like the following subjects? Put a "1" next to the one that you would most like to see offered at

```
this school, a "2" next to the one you would like second
best, and so on.  The one that you would like the least
of the five should have a "5" next to it.  No ties,
please.

____ city government                    ____ auto repair

____ introduction to computers         ____ exploring science-
                                             fiction literature
____ pottery making
```

Step 2 has provided you with information that should enable you to choose a format for your questionnaire. The steps which follow will guide you in its construction.

Step 3. Identify the frame of reference of the respondents.

In an interview, you can learn a great deal from how a person responds as well as from what he says; but when you use a questionnaire, your information is limited to the written responses. The phrasing of the questions is therefore crucial.

Before you phrase your questions, you will want to consider the frame of reference of the respondents. That is, you will want to know all you can about them so that they will understand your questions the way you intend. Here are three things you must consider:

1. *What vocabulary would be appropriate to use with this group?* In general, you will want to avoid slang, jargon, and words that have vague meanings or ambiguous interpretations. Occasionally, a slang expression will best communicate the idea of the question. If you decide to use slang, be very certain that you know exactly what the words mean *to the respondent.* Also, certain words may have the power to trigger emotional responses that make it difficult for people to attend to the actual content of a question. Try to anticipate and avoid using such words, if you can.

2. *How well informed are the respondents likely to be?* Sometimes people are perfectly willing to respond to a questionnaire, even when they know little about the subject in question. They feel they are *supposed* to know, otherwise you would not be asking them. If you suspect that some of the attitudes addressed by your questionnaire deal with matters that may be unfamiliar to some respondents, you should include lack of knowledge as a response alternative. Wording the alternative so that it does not demean the respondent (e.g., "I have not given much thought to this matter") will help respondents to admit that they lack the interest or knowledge necessary for forming an opinion.

Very often you influence people's thinking on an issue by calling their attention to it. It has been said that when you ask a question, you find out not what people think, but what they would think if asked the question. When people have strong opinions on an issue, they are, of course, less likely to be influenced by the questioning process. But if you have reason to suspect that some respondents will have little interest in the issue, be sure to provide them with the opportunity to say they have not thought about it or have no strong opinions on the subject.

3. *Does the group have a particular perspective that must be taken into account—a particular bias?* When questioning parents, for example, you will find them more thoughtful about answering questions that deal with the welfare of their own children than to questions about the general welfare of the school. Although teachers' concerns are likely to be broader, they too have better developed opinions about *personal* needs and problems. *Try to see the issue through the eyes of the respondents before you begin to ask the questions.*

Step 4. Write the questions.

As you write questions, you will need to keep foremost in mind the need to ensure the greatest possible credibility and therefore usefulness from your results.

Ensuring Useful Results

The value of your attitude questionnaire will be strongly influenced by its *emphasis,* that is, the *number of questions* you choose to ask regarding each component of the attitude objective you decided to assess while completing Step 1. A good attitude measure focuses upon a few basic attitude objectives. This will need to be the case, in particular, where the attitudes you are attempting to assess are high level ones, such as attitudes toward themselves, their classmates or co-workers, subject matter, or the school or work setting. It will be less critical in situations where you are asking simple questions which can easily be answered, such as whether students enjoyed first aid films which were given during the health period. A glance at Chapter 11, which discusses validity and reliability of attitude measures, will help you understand better the need for *several converging questions* in the assessment of a difficult-to-detect attitude. The major reason for having several questions aimed at a single attitude is instrument validity. A questionnaire which asks about slightly different aspects of the same thing several times and uses a combination of the results from these questions (an *index*) to indicate the presence of an attitude is likely to be less affected in its results by random error. Therefore, it will be more reliable. A reliable attitude instrument can support a strong case for validity, and therefore credibility. Good validity will be important if a *decision* will be based on questionnaire results, such as whether to classify a person a certain way, or change some feature of the program.

A good way to combine the results of several questions while still assessing attitudes in one questionnaire is to think of the questionnaire as a group of short attitude rating scales (see Chapter 6) in which the scores from sets of three or four questions are combined to yield a single *index* (a sum, or average score) indicating the degree of presence of a particular attitude.

Information resulting from the adding of subscores. Certain questionnaire responses can be summed to yield an index of behavior somewhat like those obtained from an attitude rating scale. The following exemplifies a situation in which you might wish to sum a set of scores for such a purpose:

Example. Teachers in a new experienced-based science program had filled out a questionnaire about each of several children in their classes. Here is a portion of the questionnaire.

Child's name _____	1 almost never	2 seldom	3 about 50% of the time	4 usually	5 almost always
1) Does this child arrive at the class or nature site promptly?					
2) Does this child listen carefully to explanations?					
3) Does this child work on assigned tasks without supervision?					
4) Does this child ask questions?					
5) Does this child volunteer for extra work?					
6) Does this child discuss science experiences with other children?					

In the course of the evaluation, teachers suggested that the experimental program worked well with children of all ability levels if they were children who became enthusiastic about the program, but that it did not work well with the children who put forth routine effort.

The evaluator therefore decided to examine program results separately for children reported as highly enthusiastic and children reported as putting forth average effort. She examined the questionnaire items and results and noted that items 2, 3, 4 and 5 were highly correlated. She summed these items on each questionnaire to get an "enthusiasm index" for each child for whom the teacher had filled out a questionnaire. Here, for example, is how one teacher answered the questions about Tom Gray:

Child's name *Tom Gray*	1 almost never	2 seldom	3 about 50% of the time	4 usually	5 almost always
1) Does this child arrive at the class or nature site promptly?				✓	
2) Does this child listen carefully to explanations?			✓		
3) Does this child work on assigned tasks without supervision?		✓			
4) Does this child ask questions?		✓			
5) Does this child volunteer for extra work?	✓				
6) Does this child discuss science experiences with other children?				✓	

Thus, the enthusiasm index for Tom was 3+2+2+1=8. The lowest possible enthusiasm index would be 4 (if every item were answered "1"), and the highest index would be 20 (if every item were answered "5").

The evaluator was able to divide students into "low enthusiasm" and "high enthusiasm" groups on the basis of the index formed by the items 2, 3, 4 and 5. This summation was perhaps better than asking for a single enthusiasm rating by teachers, since the summation represented several indicators of specific behaviors.

Once you have decided how many questions to allocate to each attitude, and whether or not to calculate attitude indices, proceed with writing questions. Use the description of the information you are attempting to obtain from this questionnaire (Step 1), your ideas for an appropriate format (Step 2), and your ideas about the frame of reference of the respondents (Step 3) to write a first draft of the questions you plan to ask. As has been mentioned, an excellent procedure to assist you in writing a first draft and selecting appropriate response choices for a closed-response questionnaire is to conduct interviews with a few respondents. Using open-ended questions in the interview, you can begin to identify the kinds of response choices you will need to include. Another way to circumvent problems with inappropriate question wording is to use questions which other people have used effectively before.

Step 5. Prepare a data summary sheet.

This step should be performed in tandem with Step 4. A data summary sheet is exactly what its name implies: it is a sheet of paper whose format, usually boxes and grids, has been designed so that all the responses from a pile of attitude instruments can be tallied or recorded in one place for summarization, future graphing or statistical analysis, and interpretation.

A data summary sheet will help you *search for patterns of responses* that allow you to characterize attitudes toward the program. It may seem odd to be concerned about how you will summarize the data at a point where you have barely decided what questions to ask. But there are two good reasons to be concerned about this problem now:

1. It is time consuming to extract information from a pile of attitude instruments and record it onto a single sheet in order to examine, summarize, and interpret it. Early attention to how this will be done can help you to better organize your efforts. Planning the data summary sheet will encourage you to eliminate unnecessary questions and make sure you are seeking answers at the appropriate level of detail for your needs.

2. Careful thought about how the information will be summarized and presented (for example, mean responses for Groups X and C) may bring to mind additional questions that should be included to render the questionnaire a more reliable measure of a certain important attitude or may suggest an organization of the data—say, by level of parents' education—that will make your results more interpretable. At this early point in instrument development, you can easily add questions or plan for a more detailed summary. Later changes may cause extra work or an unalterable loss of credibility.

The format of the data summary sheet will depend on the types of measures you have used, and whether you can take advantage of mechanical data processing.

The *type of measure* you have used will determine the ease with which you can summarize your findings. For some of the kinds of questionnaires dealt with in this chapter, as well as for interviews and observations, data summary presents special challenges. A detailed discussion of how to summarize data from such instruments appears in Chapter 12. Attitude scales, discussed in Chapter 6, are the easiest to summarize since they yield a single number per respondent. Score results from such scales can be treated as achievement test scores.

Mechanical data processing, including computer analysis of data and machine scoring of actual instruments, will either affect the format of the data summary sheet or make it unnecessary to have one at all. Since computer analysis and machine-scored testing are becoming increasingly accessible to schools and businesses it is possible that you can conserve your own time by investigating these services. Call your district research and evaluation office, or a few local data processing companies. If you find that mechanical data processing fits your time and budget constraints, then your data summary sheet will need to conform to the machine's requirements. You might even find that your questionnaire, if formatted properly, can be *read and scored* by machine, or that you can use a machine-scorable answer sheet. Your inquiry might even persuade the company or district to adopt a *general purpose* machine-scorable answer sheet to save time for everyone who must process achievement and attitude measures fast and accurately. Use of such sheets, like the one reproduced in Figure 1, has become increasingly popular.

In any case, if you plan to use machine scoring or computer data processing, discuss the format and content of your instruments with your data analyst before you write anything.

Chapter 12 describes preparation and use of data summary sheets for both hand and machine interpretation. Regardless of how you plan to summarize the data, or what type of instrument you develop, your data summary sheet should be outlined, and some of the suggestions in Chapter 12 should be considered at this early point in instrument development.

Step 6. Critique the questions; try them out and revise them.

Below is a set of criteria to help you critique your questions. For *each question* you have written, ask yourself:

1. Does the question relate to one idea? If there is more than one idea, use more than one question.
2. Is there a simpler or more direct way to ask the question? Try to keep a question under 20 words, and try to limit the number of complex concepts contained in any one question. A good rule-of-thumb is to try not to use words having three or more syllables, unless you are certain that they will be familiar to respondents.
3. Are there confusing words in the question—words that may be unfamiliar to the respondents or that may have more than one meaning or more than one pronunciation? If you are uncertain about a word and how it might be interpreted, ask various people for their interpretations.

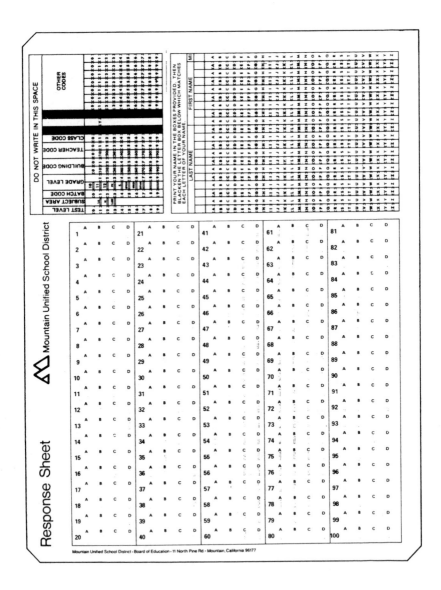

Figure 1. General purpose machine-scored answer sheet.

4. Are there words or phrases that are likely to influence a person's responses for reasons not germane to the issue? Some words make people nervous, as in this example:

Should supervisors forbid staff to leave the work area without permission?

Here is a better way to ask the same question:

Should supervisors require that staff ask permission before leaving the work area?

The next example has a phrase that presents two problems:

Do you think the teacher did the best she could to provide your child with suitable learning activities during the semester?

First, some people might respond with a "yes" because of reluctance to criticize or take a position against another person. Others could respond with a "yes" while thinking, "The poor lady did the best she could considering her limited talent!" The question is a poor one because you cannot tell what respondents are thinking. Here are questions that are more likely to obtain the desired information:

Were classroom activities at about the right level of difficulty for your child during the semester?
Were classroom activities interesting enough for your child?

5. Is the question asked negatively? For instance:

Would you prefer that your child not take part in the program?

Negative questions sometimes confuse respondents, and in some instances the negative word is overlooked. Try your best to state the question in positive terms. Then, if you decide that the question must be stated negatively, call attention to the negative word by underlining it.

6. Is the question loaded—does it encourage one answer or discourage another? There are various kinds of loaded questions. Some are quite obvious:

Are we likely to improve the program very much by spending just a little money?

And some are more subtle:

Our Board of Directors feels that . . . How do you feel about it?
Our present policy is to . . . Do you think we should change it?

The second question provides legitimacy to a particular point of view by citing an authority or prestigious person. The last question provides legitimacy to a particular point of view by identifying it with established practice and pitting it against an unknown change. *If the question seems to suggest a right or wrong answer, change it.*

7. Does the question permit a response that indicates a lack of knowledge or lack of opinion without demeaning the respondent? This criterion was discussed previously.

Once you have written a first draft, you should try it out on a sample of respondents or even on available colleagues. Tryouts are essential. They will help you uncover many problems in the formatting and phrasing of items or in the response selections.

Step 7. Assemble the questionnaire.

There are several things to be considered when assembling the questionnaire. The following suggestions may help you with this task.

Deciding on the appearance of the page. The appearance of a questionnaire is extremely important. The first impression it leaves will affect response rate. Try to make it look easy to fill out so that people will not file it away and forget about it. There should be as few questions as possible, succinctly worded, and placed on the page so that the response mode is clear. Cramming many questions into the fewest number of pages is a poor strategy. In fact, the density of the writing can discourage respondents as much as the number of pages in the questionnaire. You will have to strike some kind of balance between extra pages and crammed questions.

Use lines or skipped spaces as demarcation between blocks of questions that have different formats.

When using open-response questions, the amount of space you leave for the response will affect the length of the response. If you do not want to limit the answers, be sure to leave sufficient space or to instruct the respondents to use the backs of the pages.

When using closed-response questions, it is a good idea to provide boxes for the responses rather than just open blanks. If you have the room, double space between response categories:

```
Will you be a classroom volunteer next semester?

☐ yes

☐ no

☐ undecided
```

Deciding on the question sequence. Unless there is a special reason for randomizing the order of the questions, you should arrange them in some logical grouping—by subject matter or by request format, for example. Sometimes the way people respond to one question will influence the way they respond to subsequent questions because of their reluctance to seem inconsistent. There is no way to get around this problem entirely, but you may want to review your question order with this in mind.

Using contingency questions. Contingency questions are questions whose asking is dependent on the response to a prior question:

Did you serve as a classroom volunteer this semester?

☐ yes   ☐ no

If yes, how much of your time in the classroom was spent working directly with your own child?

☐ 25% or less   ☐ 50% - 75%

☐ 25% - 50%   ☐ over 75%

Contingency questions make it possible for some people to skip questions that do not apply to them.

Introducing the questionnaire. Introductory comments should explain the purpose of the questionnaire and provide guidelines for answering the questions:

This questionnaire is being sent to parents of children in the early childhood program (all children in grades K, 1, 2, and 3). The program has been in progress for the past year, and we would like to have your opinions to help us evaluate it. Some parents have not had direct experience with certain features of the program, so we have organized the questionnaire into two parts. *All* parents should fill in Part I. Fill in Part II if you participated as a volunteer in classroom activities; otherwise, ignore Part II.

Sometimes the questionnaire will consist of several sections. The layout of the questionnaire should make divisions between sections clear. You may wish to include an introductory comment before each section:

The purpose of this part of the questionnaire is to
find out your opinions on the value of the parent
volunteer activities.

Writing the instructions. The instructions for each type of question
should be specific and unambiguous:

Please place an X in the box by the *one* best
response.

Please feel free to continue writing on the back
of the page if you run out of room.

Aim for as simple a format as possible—one in which the response possibilities are self-explanatory. You should assume that a portion of the respondents will ignore the instructions altogether. The fact is that people do not
like to bother reading long, elaborate instructions and are more likely to
respond if they can just plunge right in. If you feel the format might be
confusing, include a conspicuous sample item at the beginning.

Mailed questionnaires. If the questionnaire is to be mailed, you may
wish to put the introductory comments in a cover letter, or in the
questionnaire itself. A *deadline* for returning the questionnaire should
always be indicated. If you can afford the time, give local respondents
about 10 days; those far away, about three weeks. Encourage the respondents to fill out the questionnaire as soon as possible. Hopefully, you will
counteract the tendency of people to file mail away and forget it.

Also keep in mind that a questionnaire on three or more sheets of
standard weight paper will need additional postage. In many cases, having
your typed copy *photographically reduced* is an inexpensive way to fit
more questions into less space. A stamped envelope should be provided, or
the questionnaire itself should be constructed so that it can be folded,
stapled, and mailed back to you without an envelope, as in Figure 2.

Group-administered questionnaires. If the questionnaire is to be given
to students in the classroom, the instructions should be given orally. For
this purpose, a single cover sheet with each set of questionnaires is
appropriate. The teacher can use the cover sheet to read instructions with
the class. Where possible, it is a good idea to tape-record instructions.

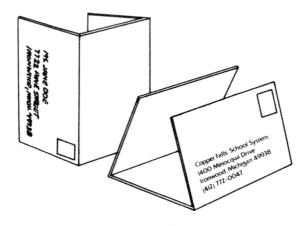

Figure 2. Two views of handy self-mailing format for short questionnaires. Printed on heavy paper, this unusual construction should encourage a good response rate. The respondent simply answers, refolds, staples, and mails.

Tryouts. When you have assembled the questionnaire and you are satisfied that it is your best effort, duplicate a few, and *try them out* with people who are as like your intended respondents as possible. Ask about criticisms and confusions. This quick but crucial step may keep you from distributing a questionnaire that contains a flaw—perhaps in wording of questions or instructions, formatting, or sequencing—that could harm your results.

Step 8. Administer the questionnaire.

The questionnaire can be given to everyone in the group or to a random sample if the total group is very large.[2] The costs involved in printing, distributing, and scoring the questionnaire may determine what you do in this regard. For example, if you have to mail the questionnaire and provide the return postage, you may decide that you cannot afford to reach the entire group. In some cases, however, the cost may be outweighed by the impact on morale of allowing everyone in the group to have his say.

Questionnaires that are mailed or sent out tend to have a low return rate. To work against this, you should probably plan on some *follow-up procedures*—for example, gently worded phone calls to those who have not responded:

I am calling to ask if you have returned the questionnaire that was sent to you. We are trying to get as large a response as possible and would appreciate your filling it out and returning it if you have not yet done so.

If you can afford a *second* mailing, send your questionnaires or a post-card reminder to non-respondents a short time after the first deadline has elapsed. To the extent that you can call attention to the fact that this is a second attempt and that questionnaire return is critical, you can significantly improve your return rate. Figure 3, which reproduces some cartoons stamped on second-mailing questionnaires, shows that a little humor persuades.

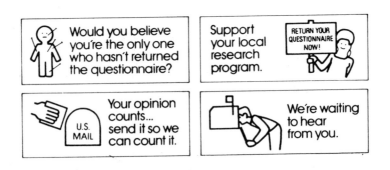

Figure 3. Stamped messages for second mailings

How do you do such a follow-up if people are to respond anonymously? One procedure is to number the return envelopes, check them off a master list as they are returned, remove the questionnaires from the envelopes, and throw the envelopes away.

When distributing any instrument, you should ask administrators to lend their support to your effort. If the instrument carries the sanction of the CEO project director or the school principal, it is more likely to receive the attention of those involved. Their request for quick returns can carry more authority than yours.

What do you do when the questionnaires have been returned? Turn to Chapter 12.

Notes

1. "Closed" and "open" response formats are referred to in the measurement literature as "selected" and "constructed," respectively. Since these terms tend to be confusing, the simpler, more descriptive ones are used here.

2. To obtain information about sampling, consult a text on the topic of experimental design or methods for survey research. One such book is *How to Design a Program Evaluation*, Volume 3 of the *Program Evaluation Kit*.

For Further Reading

Fitz-Gibbon, C. F., & Morris, L. L. (1987). *How to design a program evaluation*. Newbury Park, CA: Sage. This book is part of the *Program Evaluation Kit*. If your group is so large that you must sample, the chapter on how to randomize will be useful.

Kahn, R. L., & Cannell, C. F. (1957). *The dynamics of interviewing*. New York: John Wiley. "The Formulation of Questions" is one of the many useful chapters in this book.

Payne, S. L. (1951). *The art of asking questions*. Princeton, NJ: Princeton University Press. This is a very helpful book on how to word questions.

Weisberg, H. F., & Bowen, B. D. (1977). *An introduction to survey research and data analysis*. San Francisco: W. H. Freeman. A general text on conducting attitude surveys.

Chapter 6
Developing Your Own Measures: Attitude Rating Scales

This chapter describes three types of attitude rating scales:[1]

- The ordered scale
- The agreement scale
- The semantic differential

An attitude rating scale yields a *single score* that indicates both the direction and intensity of a person's attitude, although some scales yield "sub-scale" scores as well. For example, a rating scale designed to measure *attitude toward job satisfaction* may have a set of items that relates to attitude toward pay and benefits, another set that relates to attitude toward working conditions, and so forth. Each of these sub-sets can yield a separate score in addition to the total score. Because of the scoring methods of most attitude rating scales, each item must differentiate those respondents with a favorable attitude from those with an unfavorable attitude. In addition, the items must allow for expression of a broad range of feelings from strongly unfavorable through neutral to strongly favorable.

The guidelines provided here for constructing *ordered scales* and *agreement scales* are generally used by people involved in developing such instruments for research purposes. To follow the guidelines as they are described in this section might require more time and effort than you care to devote to this endeavor. They are included for the few who, because of some future or long-term need, want to produce a highly credible instrument.

The Ordered Scale

The ordered scale consists of a collection of statements that express a range of opinions about an attitude object:

- School teaches you things that help in getting a job.
- Most teachers deeply care about their students.
- Sometimes school can be interesting.
- School is really a bore.
- There are too many rules at school.
- School is the most valuable way I can spend my time.

Before inclusion on the measure, these statements are assigned a "scale value" along an attitude continuum by a panel of judges. An instrument is then constructed which presents the statements in random order without indicating their scale values. The respondents are asked to check those statements with which they agree. Only *opinion statements* are used. *Factual statements* are not included in this kind of measure, since people with differing attitudes could agree to a statement of fact. Note that the respondents are asked to select only those items *with which they agree* and to reject all others.

Steps for Constructing and Using an Ordered Scale

1. Accumulate a large number of statements about the attitude object (approximately 100). A good source for these statements might be interviews of prospective respondents. Make sure that the statements represent a wide range of opinion, including moderate ones.
2. Place each statement on a separate piece of paper.
3. Select a group of judges (preferably 30 or more people like the prospective respondents) and ask each one to sort the statements into 11 piles ranging from highly unfavorable (1) through neutral (6) to highly favorable (11). *Make sure the judges understand that they are classifying the statements and not indicating their agreement or disagreement with them.*
4. Throw out statements that have been placed in widely differing piles. These are ambiguous statements.
5. For each remaining statement, arrive at a scale value by computing the median or mean position of the assignments by the judges.

6. Select a set of statements (under 25) whose scale values will give you a spread that evenly covers the continuum from highly unfavorable to highly favorable.
7. Construct the questionnaire by listing the statements in *random order*. Do not indicate scale values on the instrument.
8. Administer the instrument, instructing respondents to indicate with which statements they agree.
9. Compute a score for each respondent by finding the mean of the scale values of the statements selected by that respondent.

The Agreement Scale

The more common agreement scale also consists of a series of attitude statements. Unlike the ordered scale, however, these sentences do not represent gradations of the attitude. They embody extreme statements, either clearly favorable or clearly unfavorable. The agreement scale achieves a wide range of scores by having respondents report the *intensity* of an attitude. This is accomplished by providing gradations within the response alternatives. The respondents are asked to indicate their agreement with each statement on a 5-point scale:

SA	A	U	D	SD
strongly agree	agree	undecided	disagree	strongly disagree

This question format is a familiar one that can be found in a variety of measures, not just attitude rating scales. It is a popular multiple-choice format that is frequently used in the construction of many types of attitude questionnaires.

Steps for Constructing and Using an Agreement Scale

1. Accumulate a large number of clearly favorable or clearly unfavorable statements about the attitude you wish to measure (approximately 60). As with the statements for the ordered scale, a good source might be prospective respondents.
2. Ask a *pilot* group (50 or more) to respond to these statements. The pilot group should consist of people who are (a) similar to the people whose attitudes you wish to measure, and (b) likely to express the whole range of attitudes you wish the instrument to detect.

3. Score responses by assigning them from one to five points—five for most favorable, one for least favorable. This, of course, means responses will be scored differently depending on whether the statement reflects a negative or positive attitude.

Example. Scoring key for two items measuring attitude toward school.

School is a waste of time.

School teaches you things that help in getting a job.

SA A U D SD
1   2 3 4 5

SA A U D SD
5   4 3 2 1

Note that the highest rating (5) for favorable attitude toward school may be given to strongly disagree (SD) or to strongly agree (SA) depending on how the item is worded.

---

4. Compute a score for each respondent by totaling the points corresponding to his or her responses.
5. Identify high scorers (top 25%) and low scorers (lowest 25%).
6. Analyze each statement according to how high and low scorers responded to it. The method for accomplishing this step, called "item analysis," is discussed below.
7. Retain those items (approximately 20) which provided good discrimination between high and low scorers.
8. Construct the questionnaire by listing the retained statements in random order.
9. Administer the instrument.
10. Compute a score for each respondent by totaling the scores corresponding to his or her responses.

Item analysis. In measurement texts, statistical techniques of item analysis are described for making comparisons between how respondents performed on individual items and how they scored on the instrument as a whole. *The purpose for doing an item analysis is to select from a pool of items the ones that most effectively obtain the information you want, and to eliminate the less effective items from your instrument.* You can perform an informal analysis by the method demonstrated below:

Example. An agreement scale containing 60 items has been administered to eighty respondents. Twenty high and twenty low scorers (i.e., the top and bottom 25% of the eighty respondents) have been identified using steps 3, 4, and 5 given above. The completed instruments from these forty respondents are examined, and their responses on each item are tabulated as follows:

Item No.	20 high scorers' response choices					20 low scorers' response choices				
	SA	A	U	D	SD	SA	A	U	D	SD
1	|		|||	卌 ||	卌 ||||	卌 |||	卌 卌	||		
2	||||	|||	卌	|||	卌	|||	|||	卌 ||	|||	||||
3	||	|||	卌	卌 |	||||	卌	卌	卌	||	|||
4	卌	卌 |||	||||	|	|	||		|||	卌 ||	卌 |||

etc. to 60

The letters on the horizontal axis represent the possible response choices for each item. The numbers on the vertical axis represent the item number. By placing in one pile the responses of high scorers (those whose total score fell in the upper 25% range) and in a second pile the responses of low scorers (those whose total score fell in the lower 25% range), the evaluator can make a quick tally of how the people in both these groups responded to each item. From this information it can be determined which items contributed most to the difference in responses between high and low scorers. Such items are "good discrimination" items and should be retained.

Item 2 should be thrown out, since the response patterns of high and low scorers are almost identical. Item 3 is marginal. It may or may not be included, depending on whether there are a sufficient number of items that do a better job. Items 1 and 4 seem to be doing a good job of differentiating between high and low scorers. They should be checked to determine whether the assignment of points to their response alternatives corresponds to the overall questionnaire. In order for item 1 to be retained, for example, "SD" must be a response that receives 5 points. If this is the case, then high scorers are scoring high on item 1. Item 4, however, has an opposite scoring pattern. In order to be retained, it must allot "SD" only 1 point. If item 4 gives "SD" 5 points, then it has a scoring pattern in the reverse direction to the overall questionnaire, and it should be discarded.

The Semantic Differential

This scale consists of a series of adjectives and their antonyms listed on opposite sides of the page with seven "attitude positions" in between. At the top of the page, the attitude object is named as the heading. The attitude object may be stated as a word, a phrase, or it may even be a picture. For example:

```
                          fitness
    bad    ___  ___  ___  ___  ___  ___  ___    good

   fair    ___  ___  ___  ___  ___  ___  ___    unfair

  right    ___  ___  ___  ___  ___  ___  ___    wrong
```

The semantic differential is generally regarded as a good tool for measuring *affect*—people's positive and negative *feelings* toward an attitude object. Its score represents the respondent's general impression about the attitude object. Because of this, it is useful in situations where people are likely to have strong emotional reactions to a topic but not well thought out opinions. Since this will not often be the case in program evaluation and since the semantic differential yields only general impressions without information about their source, it is not often worth the effort expended.

There is controversy, in addition, among educational researchers as to the value of this kind of instrument for use with young children. Some maintain that children are not able to respond to gradated questions that use lines or points to indicate degrees of difference. Others maintain that stability can be found in the responses of children as young as third grade, especially if the scales use the vocabulary of the children who will respond to them.

DiVesta (1965) has developed scales to use with children from the inner city. The following are some of the adjective pairs contained in his scales.

positive	negative	positive	negative
good	bad	fast	slow
friendly	unfriendly	first	last
pretty	ugly	sharp	dull
right	wrong	brave	not brave
sweet	sour	strong	weak
funny	sad	new	old

Steps for Constructing and Using a Semantic Differential

1. Determine the attitude object(s) you wish to investigate.
2. Select appropriate adjective pairs (approximately 10). You may wish to select from the list provided at the end of this chapter or from DiVesta's list if it suits your participants. You may, on the other hand, wish to make up your own list.
3. Write the attitude-object word or phrase at the top of the page and place the adjectives beneath it. If you are examining more than one attitude object, use the same adjective order for each attitude object, and keep the words in the same position. Provide "random polarity." This means that the adjective pairs should *not* be listed so that all positive responses fall on one side and all negative responses on the other.

Example

How do you feel about each of these subjects? Place an X on one of the seven lines between each pair.

physical exercise

bad	___	___	___	___	___	___	___	good
friendly	___	___	___	___	___	___	___	unfriendly
fair	___	___	___	___	___	___	___	unfair
sour	___	___	___	___	___	___	___	sweet

art

bad	___	___	___	___	___	___	___	good
friendly	___	___	___	___	___	___	___	unfriendly
fair	___	___	___	___	___	___	___	unfair
sour	___	___	___	___	___	___	___	sweet

---

4. Instruct the respondents about how and where to mark their ratings. They should be instructed to respond quickly and on the basis of their first impressions. You may find that some people are not comfortable responding to a concept (e.g., physical exercise, art) with seemingly inappropriate adjectives (e.g., sweet/sour). You will have to reassure such people that this type of scale calls for *impressions*, not studied responses. If you are using the instrument with children, you would do well to give them some practice with other concepts (attitude objects) before they make their ratings on the concepts you want to measure.

5. Compute a person's score by assigning a "1" to responses indicating the most negative response, a "7" to the most positive response, and scoring intermediate responses from "2" to "6" accordingly. A person's score for any one attitude object is the average of responses to the attitude pairs.

Here are more adjective pairs you might use for constructing semantic differential rating scales:

negative	positive	negative	positive
boring	interesting	unhealthy	healthy
uninformative	informative	dull	lively
confusing	clear	weak	strong
irrelevant	relevant	unfair	fair
superficial	profound	dirty	clean
biased	objective	worthless	valuable
purposeless	purposeful	useless	useful
closed	open	passive	active
tense	relaxed	static	dynamic
unhappy	happy	unfriendly	friendly
angry	calm	wrong	right
cold	warm		

Note

1. The steps given in this chapter for constructing the three types of attitude rating scales are adapted from Edwards and Porter (1972). In the Edwards-Porter article the three scales are referred to as the Thurstone, Likert, and Osgood scales. These are the names of the men who developed them.

For Further Reading

Fitz-Gibbon, C. T., & Morris, L. L. (1987). *How to analyze data.* Newbury Park, CA: Sage. This booklet, part of the *Program Evaluation Kit,* explains, among other things, how to calculate means and medians.

Edwards, A. L., & Porter, B. C. (1972). *The affective domain.* Washington, DC: National Special Media Institutes, Gryphon House. This book provides a more detailed discussion of the three types of measurement described in this chapter.

Chapter 7
Developing Your Own Measures: Interviews

This chapter provides suggestions to help you design and conduct effective interviews. These suggestions are organized according to the following nine steps:

1. Identify the attitude objective(s); determine what useful information the interview might provide about program effects.
2. Decide on the structure and approach of the interview.
3. Decide on the number and sequence of questions.
4. Draft questions and critique them.
5. Decide how you will summarize and report the interview data.
6. Add the introduction and probes, and choose a recording method.
7. Select the interviewer(s) and conduct a few tryouts.
8. Prepare the interviewer(s).
9. Make arrangements for the interviews.

Step 1. Identify the attitude objective(s); determine what useful information the interview might provide about program effects.

In the following example, the evaluator begins from a program goal or objective that has been spelled out in detail. Interviewing the children will be one of the methods for obtaining the necessary information.

Example

Program objective: The children will express positive attitudes toward the new after-school recreation program, specifically:

1. Participation will increase.
2. The children will express a preference for the new method of structuring activities.
3. They will report satisfaction with the new facilities.
4. The number of interpersonal conflicts will decline.

Information to be obtained from the interview:

1. Which play facilities do the children use?
2. Which facilities are not used? Why not?
3. Do the children feel there are sufficient facilities?
4. How do they react to the structuring of activities?
5. Do they prefer the structure to the previous unstructured situation?
6. Are the children encountering fewer problems than they did previously?
7. What kinds of problems do they encounter?
8. Are the problems different from the ones they encountered earlier, or are they the same?
9. Do the children use the play yard more or less than they used to? Why?

Step 2. Decide on the structure and approach of the interview.

Degree of Structure

An interview can be *unstructured*, much like an ordinary conversation between two people:

Tell me, what do you think about the Humane Society's pet visiting program at this nursing home? We're interested in finding out if you and the other residents like it and if you want it to continue next year.

An *unstructured* interview, like a conversation, takes its own course. Though the interviewer may have a general notion of topics to be covered, the encounter follows a direction determined then and there.

On the other hand, an interview can be *highly* structured, as though two people were sitting down to fill out a questionnaire together:

> *I'm going to ask you a series of questions about the new fitness program. We're interested in finding out . . . etc. About how many times last week did you use the facilities? Which of these activities did you take part in? . . . Do you like the new program?*

The interview that is highly structured has a definite agenda: a set of questions to be covered, and often a fixed sequence in which they are to be asked.

Your decisions concerning the amount of structure will be influenced by the information you seek and the skill of your interviewer. If you know with some precision the kind of information you want, then you can structure your questions in order to elicit that information. If you are less certain of what you are likely to find when you start asking questions, then you might prefer a looser structure.

Often the critical determiner of the amount of structure of an interview is the experience of the interviewers. If yours are inexperienced, you should probably provide them with detailed instructions and structure question sequences as much as possible.

Surveys and polls are generally highly structured and consist of questions that call for short, easily recorded responses.

Open or Closed Questions?

Once you have settled on the issue of structure, decide on a question type. Do you wish to use general (open) questions that allow for a wide range of responses, or do you wish to use specific (closed) questions that direct the answers? Unstructured interviews nearly always demand open questions, but a structured interview can contain open questions, closed questions, or both. Open questions elicit a variety of responses; closed questions call for specific responses. Broader questions permit greater flexibility and are useful when the issue under investigation is complex. More specific questions sometimes channel people's responses, even when the people have no opinion on the subject. If confronted with a question like this, "Do you agree that teachers should make all student placement decisions?" people are apt to respond with a yes or no even though they may never have thought about it before.

When possible, take advantage of the flexibility that an interview allows you by providing questions that give people room to respond. Whether you use general questions, specific ones, or a combination of general and specific questions, *make sure that each question deals with only one idea.*

Starting with an open-ended, general question and then following it up with several specific questions is often a good way to enjoy the best of both worlds.

Direct or Indirect Approach?

The interview approach can be direct or indirect. The above examples use a direct approach. They explain the purpose of the interview, and they direct attention to the area of concern. An indirect approach states the interview's purpose more vaguely. Here is an example of this approach based on the program objective defined above about an after-school recreation program:

> *I'm trying to find out about some things that kids like to do in their spare time. What are some of the things that you do for fun in your spare time? When do you have the most time to play? Do you happen to live within walking distance of the school? . . .*

Sometimes an indirect approach is used to reduce the influence that the interview situation might have on a person's responses. When the student freely volunteers, without being asked directly, the chances are that he really means it and is not simply saying so because it is what he thinks the interviewer wants to hear.

An indirect approach is also used when a more direct approach would be perceived as threatening to the respondent or when the respondent does not have the knowledge necessary to respond to direct questions, as is sometimes the case with very young children. Unless you can justify using an indirect approach, though, it is more honest to use the direct approach.

Step 3. Decide on the number and sequence of questions.

Use as many questions as you need to get the information. You will do better to err in the direction of asking too many questions, especially with questions related to important objectives.

The question sequence can move from general to specific if you want to give people an opportunity to begin by responding without restriction. Or the question sequence can move from specific to general if you feel that people are not likely to have given the subject much thought. Their answers to specific questions could then guide them through the process of organizing their thinking on the subject.

Questions should follow one another with some logical sequence that is inherent in the subject under consideration. If the interviewer jumps about from one subject to another, the respondents can become confused or annoyed. When it is necessary to change topics, instruct the interviewer to provide transitional statements to help the respondent make the change, such as, "Now let's talk about something else."

Step 4. Draft questions and critique them.

Whether you are framing questions for a structured or an unstructured interview, be sure to keep in mind the frame of reference of your respondents. Remember that your interview will ask them to probe their personal experience and express their own wants and needs. Every question you ask should be appropriate to its audience. As you generate questions for the interview, you will want to ask yourself:

- What are their interests?
- What topics relevant to the interview are they likely to have formed opinions about beforehand?
- What information pertinent to the topic are they likely to have?
- What vocabulary and phrases will they understand?

In the following question asked of a group of parents, both the language and the frame of reference are inappropriate:

The city schools define individualization as "the differentiation of instruction to best serve the individual needs of a pupil." Does this describe your child's current school experience?

It is unlikely that most parents would know how to respond to the question since it uses educational terms whose meanings are imprecise even to educators. In addition, the question fails to focus on the critical issue: Does the parent feel his child is doing assignments at about the right level of difficulty, and taking part in classroom activities that serve the child's particular educational needs? Here are the kinds of questions one might use to elicit the desired information:

- *What do you think Linda needed to work on at school this semester?*
- *Was there any special subject or skill that you felt she needed special help with?*
- *Did Linda show you her assignments or talk much about what she did in class?*
- *Do you think Linda's assignments were right for her? Do you think they provided her with practice in what she needed?*
- *Did Linda feel she could get help when she needed it?*

Once you have written your questions, critique them using the guidelines for examining questions for questionnaires in Chapter 5, page 75.

Step 5. Decide how you will summarize and report the interview data.

This step requires that you design a method for summarizing the information you collect, reducing it to a form that can be looked at all at once.

This will help you to search for patterns among the attitudes that have been expressed.

Though it may seem odd to be concerned about how you will summarize the data before you have conducted the interviews, there are good reasons why this step is critical now:

1. It is time-consuming to summarize large bodies of orally given information. Planning how this will be done now will help you prevent wasted effort. You will be able to eliminate unnecessary questions and make sure you are seeking answers at the appropriate level of detail for your needs.

2. You may decide to report results separately for different categories of respondents, and this may create a need for additional information. For instance, if you are interested in measuring employees' attitudes toward an in-service training program, and you decide to report results separately for those who participated in a previous workshop, then you will need to ask an additional question about their past participation.

What method you use to summarize interview data will be determined by the types of questions you have decided to ask. If you have opted to conduct unstructured interviews, then the answers you will record will probably take the form of open-reponse data—notes or transcribed conversation. If the interview will be structured, then your data will consist of closed responses, which can be as specific as check-marked, multiple-choice answers. A combination of question types is another possibility.

If you will have closed-response data, then plan to treat your interview recording sheets exactly as you would closed-response questionnaires. Refer to page 73 of this booklet, and design a *data summary sheet.* You should then refer to Chapter 12 and consider mechanical scoring, computer data processing, or formatting the interview recording sheet for direct keypunching.

In the more likely event that your interview data will contain open-response answers, there are two kinds of summaries: a *paragraph* that describes general opinions, or a set of *numerical values,* based on some categorization scheme, that can be tabulated and used in further summaries and statistical analyses. Chapter 12 should help you decide on a summary method or methods. It also guides you with step-by-step directions for each.

Step 6. Add the introduction and probes, and choose a recording method.

The introduction should be very carefully planned. It should be designed to make the respondents comfortable so that they will be motivated to respond to the questions that follow. A logical way to begin is to describe (1) the purpose of the interview, (2) the ways in which the information will be used, and (3) what will be expected of the respondent. Inherent in this approach is the idea that the respondents' opinions are important and might bring about desirable consequences. Explaining what will be expected of the respondents will help to alleviate the worries that are an inevitable part of the interview situation. If information can be kept confidential, for instance, say so.

You can prevent misleading results by giving adequate introductory information to each person interviewed. For example, Michael who stays after school each day for crafts may mistakenly think that the after-school recreation program you are questioning him about consists solely of the handball game that occurs daily on the other side of the yard. You might find it useful to provide standard explanations and *definitions* to ensure that crucial ideas are understood.

After you have developed the questions and organized them, try out the interview on a sample of respondents. These tryouts will help to identify the questions which will require probes.

Probes are a necessary part of any interview. They are questions that elicit additional information in the case of incomplete or vague answers. There are various reasons why a respondent might answer incompletely. The most likely are:

- They might not be able to remember all the information that you have requested.
- They might have a different frame of reference than your question implies.

For instance, if you asked a teacher about the level of student interest in an environmental education class and the teacher answered that interest seemed low, a probe might give you information to the contrary:

Probe: *Is student interest higher or lower or the same as it used to be?*

Answer: *Oh, it's much higher than it used to be. It's just not as high as I expected.*

This response changes your idea of the outcomes of the program. Because of the probe, the interviewer has obtained a more realistic picture of what actually occurred.

There is no format into which you can set probes. At times, good ways of probing to gain more complete information from respondents who have forgotten or left something out of their answer might be to simply say:

- *I see. Is there anything else?*
- *How do you mean?*
- *I'd like to know more about your thinking on that.*
- *Why do you think that happened?*
- *Can you explain that a little more?*

Your probes might also focus on a specific word or phrase. Try to take notes during an unstructured interview, and while the respondent is in the process of answering, design questions or probes to ask immediately afterwards.

You should, for example, insert probes whenever the respondent makes a strong statement in either an expected or an unexpected direction. For instance, the teacher queried above might have said:

> *Oh yes. Student interest is very high—100%. Everyone loves the program.*

The best probe for such a strong response is a simple rephrasing and repetition:

> *Your statement is that every student is happy with the program 100% of the time?*

This probe leads the respondent to reconsider a strong statement and thereby gives her a chance to give more accurate information. Notice that this particular probe is a non-directive restatement of what the respondent answered, rather than a statement of doubt or of incredulity such as:

> *You mean absolutely nobody dislikes it ever?*

Here again, be aware of the possibility of putting the respondent on the defensive. A statement of doubt or incredulity sounds like a challenge to the honesty of the respondent.

The subject of honesty also enters the picture when respondents withhold information because of notions of social desirability or because of reluctance to answer in a certain way. In these situations, it appears that no amount of probing will change the response. However, to the extent that you can make an interview situation less threatening, you open up the possibility of more honest answers, regardless of social or other implications that might deter a respondent.

Before you administer any interviews, decide which *recording method* you will use. You may opt to record an interview on audiotape to be transcribed at a later time by a secretary or staff volunteer. Such recording will give you the fullest possible data, but it will involve much time on the part of the transcriber. Consequently, you should only use audiotape if you have a lot of secretarial time available to you. At best, to type out the tape in full will take the transcriber half again as long as the duration of the interview itself. If your recorded interviews are transcribed, you will be able to summarize the interview using exact quotes from the respondent. There is no question but that exact quotes from the respondents are the fairest way of reporting information they have given to you.

However, if you are in the more common situation of having little transcription help available, you will have to take notes during the interview. Most people find—and you can try this out during a practice interview—that taking notes is not really disruptive. A good thing to do is to take down only key phrases and features of the respondent's answers while you are conducting the interview. Then, *immediately after the respondent has left*, write out the full answers in as close to the person's exact words as you can reconstruct. In this situation, shortly after you record or summarize the information, show the summary to the respondent to correct any misunderstanding that you might have incorporated in your note-taking.

Step 7. Select the interviewer(s) and conduct a few tryouts.

Before selecting the interviewer, try to anticipate the ways in which the choice of interviewer might affect the results of the interview. For example, if you are asking pupils how they like a class, then obviously someone other than the teacher who taught the class should pose the questions. If you are asking employees about a program, you will probably want someone other than their supervisor to pose the questions. If you are using an oral procedure to overcome problems stemming from language difficulties, you, of course, need someone who speaks the appropriate language. If you are investigating attitudes toward racial relations, your respondents are more apt to express their honest feelings to a person of their own race. The rule of thumb is this: *People speak more freely to an interviewer whom they perceive to be like themselves*; they are less apt to distort their responses if they do not feel they are being judged or that their responses can in some way do them, or others, injury.

Whether you choose to prepare a structured or unstructured interview, you *must* rehearse it. You should give the interview once or twice to whomever is available—a wife, a husband, an older child, a secretary, or a staff member who is willing to volunteer. This dry-run procedure is a test of both the interview as you have written it and of the interviewer's ability to administer it. Generally, the things to look for are:

- Inconsistency in the logic of question sequencing
- Difficult or threateningly worded questions

Advise the person who is playing the role of respondent to be as uncooperative as possible. This attitude will prepare you for unanticipated answers and for reluctant respondents, people unwilling to give you the information you need. After one or two practice interviews, make revisions if this appears necessary to get results. A major advantage of the practice interview is that it will help you decide which answers you will have to pursue further and probe, and which ones you will be able to accept as given.

Step 8. Prepare the interviewer(s).

Make sure that the interviewers practice. Unless your interviewer has had a wealth of experience, you will probably want to spell out the interview sequence in detail, providing the interviewer with the questions to be asked and suggestions for the kinds of responses that should be pursued further.

There are some situations where you will want to withhold certain information from the interviewer. If, for example, your evaluation design calls for a comparison of responses from an experimental and a control group, you should arrange it so that the interviewer does not know which people are from which group. This technique, called "blind" interviewing, will add to the credibility of your results.

You should alert the interviewer to the kinds of behaviors that tend to inhibit respondents, such as interrupting, disagreeing, and frowning. In using probes, the interviewer should be as neutral as possible. They are designed to request further information, not to carry an emotional load.

The interviewer should also have a plan for dealing with reluctant respondents. Several reasons could account for respondents' reluctance: they might be defensive; they might be busy; they might not see a need for taking time to take part in an interview. The best way to overcome resistance is for the interviewer to be explicit and completely open about the interview and what it will demand of the respondent, perhaps giving a sample question.

Another problem the interviewer might come up against is that of "dumping." The "dumper" is a person who, through frustration or excessive enthusiasm, has been eagerly waiting for just such an occasion to speak on this topic and anything related to it. The best way to solve the problem of "dumping" is to allow the respondent time to speak his or her piece, deriving as much information relevant to the interview from the statements being made. At some point, however, it will become necessary to say "Yes, this is important information; but I also need to know such and such and time is growing short." Hopefully, it will be possible to redirect the course of the conversation. The interviewer should be careful not to express agreement with any statement made by an overzealous respondent. Support tends to guide the interview and the respondent's answers in the direction of the point of view that was supported and will thereby diminish the possibility of obtaining other kinds of information during the rest of the interview. The interviewer should take notes freely while an overzealous respondent is talking. In fact, it may be best with such a person to abandon altogether the format you had set down for the interview. The interviewer can go over notes later and fill in the interview schedule with the information received. The respondent should receive a copy of the completed schedule, with a request that he correct errors and fill in information that the interview omitted.

Step 9. Make arrangements for the interviews.

If the respondent is to come to the interviewer, be sure to provide a quiet, comfortable atmosphere in which the interview can be conducted. Allow sufficient time for each interview, keeping in mind that some people may come late and some interviews may take longer than others. The interviewer will need sufficient time between interviews to work on notes and summarize the information.

You might wish to arrange the situation so that the person already interviewed does not enter into conversation with the person who is waiting for an interview.

For Further Reading

Kahn, R. R., & Cannell, C. F. (1957). *The dynamics of interviewing.* New York: John Wiley.

Chapter 8
Developing Your Own Measures: Written Reports

Written reports essentially are lengthy responses to a set of open-ended questions. When you ask for written reports, you expect the reporter to know about the attitudes and behaviors of the subject because of some past or ongoing relationship. Written reports have the advantage of avoiding problems of instrument design or selection. Helpful also is the fact that some of these reports can be directly incorporated into the final evaluation report: they can be inserted into the text or included in an appendix.

Disadvantages of requesting reports are twofold: the difficulty of systematically interpreting the information contained in the reports, and the resistance you are likely to encounter when you ask respondents to express themselves in writing. These disadvantages make the use of written reports in attitude measurement rare. Should you wish to solicit reports, this chapter provides some guidance for their development and interpretation. It is organized according to the following five steps:

1. Identify the program objective for which the written reports will be solicited; determine what specific information you want.
2. Decide how many reports you will need, and select respondents.
3. Design the report request.
4. Distribute the report requests.
5. Summarize the reports for inclusion in your final report.

Step 1. Identify the program objective for which the written report will be solicited; determine what specific information you want.

The evaluator in the following example is attempting to determine the social and attitudinal outcomes of an affirmative action program in which a number of women and minorities were hired into six product develop-ment teams at a major corporation. In addition to collecting sociometric and self-report information from the employees, he also plans to ask the six team leaders to report on the team social dynamics and to estimate the social consequences of the program. Although the example we use is from the business world, the procedures are helpful in guiding the use of reports in any context.

Example

Program objective: By the end of the year, the new employees will feel comfortable and accepted in their new environment. Friendship pat-terns will reflect their acceptance and integration into the company.

Information to be obtained from the team leader reports: A descrip-tion of the initial and final status of the team in terms of

- friendship patterns
- small groups and cliques (rivalries? factions? confrontations?)
- cohesiveness of the team as a whole

and an assessment of the social consequences of the program. Of par-ticular interest is supporting evidence (including anecdotes) for the team leader's appraisal. This could include descriptions of positive and negative encounters among employees and synopses of statements made by individuals throughout the year that mirror presence or absence of interracial and cross-sex understanding.

Step 2. Decide how many reports you will need, and select respondents.

Consider the questions that will determine this: Will the audience of your evaluation accept reports from a fraction of the possible respondents, in which case you will be able to *sample*, or will it demand reports from everyone? How accurate do *you* feel your data will be if only a small random sample of respondents are asked to report? Random sampling from the relevant groups (e.g., employees, team leaders) will reduce the bulk of the data you collect. It will also burden fewer people with the task of writing reports.

Make a list of the respondents who could be asked to write reports. Randomly select names from the list if you have concluded that you will not need reports from all. If you decide to ask for single reports from pairs or groups, determine which members will constitute each group.

Step 3. Design the report request.

Write out a detailed description of what you want in the report, and then try out your first version of the instructions on some potential reporters to answer questions and to remove ambiguities or confusions in the instructions. As you frame your instructions, think ahead to the time when you will be reading the reports and attempting to make judgments based on the information they provide.

Sample Instructions

As you know, we are conducting an evaluation of the hiring program currently in operation. When the final report is submitted in July, we will need to describe how well the employees seem to have accepted the new situation. We are particularly interested in to what extent the new employees are becoming part of the team and company social structure.

As part of the evaluation of the hiring program, we will be asking you to prepare two brief reports (two to five pages long) describing the social patterns in the team, the first now (in October) and the second in May. In preparing your May report, we would prefer that you do *not* refer to the October report, but rather that you observe and describe the social patterns as they exist at that time, as though this were the first time you were preparing such a report. At the conclusion of your May report, we would appreciate your listing what you consider to have been the major social consequences of the program. More discussion of the May report will be included in the request we'll circulate then.

For now, when you prepare your report, please be specific, and use examples. Here are some questions that indicate the type of information we want:

- Are there close friendships? Whom do they involve?
- What kinds of groups have emerged—social, work, sports? Who are the leaders? Are there any loners? Are there group rivalries, cliques, factions? Have there been individual or group confrontations? How frequent and how serious have they been? Describe them.
- Have there been occasions in which feelings of loyalty to the team or company as a whole were engendered? When, and under what circumstances?
- Do the group social patterns shift and change frequently, or do they seem to be fairly stable?
- Can you describe specific incidents—things that employees said or did—to support your perceptions?

Step 4. Distribute the report requests.

A person in authority, such as the project director or the school principal, may help you by distributing your report requests in their name as well as yours. This may increase the likelihood that the requests will be honored. It may be necessary to supplement the initial request for reports with periodic memos reminding dilatory report writers of impending deadlines.

Step 5. Summarize the Reports for Inclusion in Your Final Report

Once you have collected the reports, write a summary of the information they contain for inclusion in the final report. This summary can be accomplished in different ways, depending on your purposes. The more usual way is to write a synopsis of the most commonly expressed opinions and observations in paragraph form, quoting extensively from the reports themselves. Step-by-step directions for this appear below. You may, however, wish to classify the reports in some way according to the opinions expressed and use this classification in statistical analyses. This might be the case, for instance, if you wished to correlate employees' productivity with the level of team leaders' confidence in a new program. You would first need to assign numerical "confidence ratings" to administrators' reports. Directions for converting unstructured written responses into numerical or categorical data appear in Chapter 12, page 170.

Summarizing a Large Number of Written Reports

If you are in the position of having to collect five or more written reports, you will want a systematic way to summarize the information found in the reports. The following procedure is offered as one possible way to do this.

1. Obtain several sheets of plain paper to use as tally sheets. Divide each paper into about four cells by drawing lines.

2. Select one of the reports, and look for the opinions and kinds of situations or events it includes. As soon as an opinion or event is described, write a short summary of it in a cell on one of the tally sheets. In one corner of the cell, tally a "|" to indicate that that statement has been made in one report. As you read the rest of the report, every time you come upon a previously unmentioned event or opinion, summarize it in a cell and give it a single tally for having appeared in one report.

3. Read the rest of the reports in any order. Record *new* statements as above. When you come upon one that *seems to have been mentioned in a previous report,* find the cell that summarizes it. Read carefully, making sure that it is pretty much the same opinion or the same kind of event. Record another "|" in the cell to show that it has been mentioned in another report. If some *part* of an event or opinion differs substantially from or adds a significant element to the first, write a statement that covers this different aspect in another cell so that you may tally the number of reports in which this new element appears.

4. Prepare summaries of the most frequent statements for inclusion in your report. There may be good reasons for recording separately data from different groups if the reporters faced circumstances that were predicted at the outset of the evaluation to bring about different results (e.g., different grade levels, different programs). Also, if the quantity of the data that you are gleaning from the reports appears to be unwieldy, you may find it necessary to organize the opinions or behaviors into different—in some cases more general, in others more narrow—categories. Whenever new summary categories are formed, however, you are cautioned to avoid the blunder of trying to cumulate the previous tallies from the original categories. The only safe procedure is to return to the original source, the reports themselves, and then tally results for the new categories.

Chapter 9
Developing Your Own Measures: Observation Procedures

Observations have the following characteristics: One or more observers are placed in a natural setting at a specified time and for a prescribed length of time. The observers are guided in their observations by some form of pre-instruction from the evaluator. Usually the observers are not associated with the program.

Although explanations and examples are confined to observations in the classroom, the procedures recommended in this chapter will be helpful in guiding data collection through observations in any context. It is assumed that you are interested in detecting behaviors that imply particular attitudes as a means of establishing whether a program is meeting objectives concerned with effective attitude change.

The information in this chapter is organized according to the following steps:

1. Identify the program objectives; determine what specific information you want.
2. Decide on the most appropriate way to obtain the information:
   Procedure 1—Systematic Observation (highly structured)
   Procedure 2—Anecdotal Records (semi-structured)
   Procedure 3—Observation by Experts (unstructured)
3. Select and prepare the observers and, if you are using an observation instrument, develop it.
4. Decide on who will be observed and when.
5. Make the necessary arrangements.

Step 1. Identify the program objectives; determine what specific information you want.

The evaluator in the following example has obtained agreement from all concerned that only an observation procedure will provide persuasive evidence of the achievement of the objectives.

Example

Program objective: The children will learn helping behaviors. They will develop concern for one another and a sense of responsibility for one another.

Information to be obtained: The program calls for multigrade classrooms in which older children are encouraged to help younger children. The theory is that such classrooms can have various benefits--cognitive as well as social. These are the questions to be answered:

1. Have the children, in fact, learned to help one another?
2. Do they help willingly? Frequently? Regularly?
3. How do they help one another? What is the quality of that help?
4. Are the helping activities initiated by the teacher or by the children?
5. Do all the children engage in helping behavior or only some?
6. Does the teacher encourage and reward helping behavior?
7. Does such behavior occur more regularly and frequently in a program classroom (as compared with a non-program classroom)?
8. Have the helping behaviors of the children in these classrooms increased over time?
9. Have the giving and receiving of help become a natural part of the classroom interaction?

Step 2. Decide on the most appropriate way to obtain the information.

Table 3 which follows describes three observation procedures. This chart separates the roles of evaluator and observer, although there will be times when the evaluator and the observer are one and the same person. The three procedures described in Table 3 differ primarily in the degree of latitude they allow the observer. Procedure 1 specifies precise behaviors to be observed. Procedure 2 provides categories of behaviors to be observed. Procedure 3 requires that the observer make all decisions regarding relevant behaviors to be observed. The question you must answer is which of these procedures is best for you.

The evaluator mentioned in the previous helping-behaviors example might use any of the three procedures. Here is how he might consider the reasons for using each one.

Procedure 1, the highly structured procedure:

Since the program defines the helping behaviors clearly and in great detail, I will construct an observation instrument for tallying the frequency of those behaviors. I'll then train observers in the use of the instrument (i.e., in identifying the behaviors described in the instrument) and send them into program and non-program classrooms at various times during the program. The information they collect will allow me to make comparisons between program and non-program classrooms and to see if the appropriate behavior increases over time.

Procedure 2, the semi-structured procedure:

Since I'm not in a position to describe these activities and behaviors in great detail, I'll ask an observer to prepare anecdotal accounts of whatever helping behaviors they discover in the course of their observations. And should I, at some future time, wish to prepare an observation instrument (Procedure 1), I can use these anecdotal accounts to help me do this.

Procedure 3, the unstructured procedure employing an expert observer:

Since a major goal of the program is to instill attitudes that result in a variety of helping activities and behaviors, and since I'm not in a position to describe these activities and behaviors in great detail, I will find an expert observer who should be able to detect these helping activities and behaviors.

As you can see, there are several factors that will influence your choice, the most important being how much time (and, of course, money) you have, what kinds of observers are available, and how specifically you can describe the behaviors you hope to see occurring.

If you can define the behaviors you are looking for with some precision, and if you have the time to develop an observation instrument and instruct observers in its use, use Procedure 1. Procedure 1 has three important advantages:

1. You need not depend upon finding experienced observers—people who have special skills or training in the attitudinal area you are evaluating.
2. You can make a check on the quality of the information you are getting. If you use two observers for even some of the observations, an estimate of the reliability of their observations can be made by com-

	Procedure 1 Systematic Observation (Highly Structured)
Who is the observer?	The observer can be anyone who can be taught to use the observation instrument.
Who determines the behavior to be observed?	The behavior to be observed is defined by the evaluator who also designs the observation instrument. The observer is given detailed instructions in how to recognize the relevant behavior.
Who decides on the number of observations and the length of time of each observation?	The evaluator makes these decisions when the observation instrument is designed or developed.
What does the observer do?	The observer: • waits for a specific behavior to occur and then records the occurrence of that behavior or the frequency of its occurrence, using an *on-the-spot checklist,* or • keeps a running account to the behaviors as they occur, recording them with the use of a code system provided by the evaluator, called a *coded behavior record,* or • reports on the behavior immediately after a period of observation. The *delayed report instrument* is a questionnaire, rating sheet or checklist. It is either filled out at the end of an extended observation period, or the observation period is broken up so that every few minutes observers alternate between observing and recording what was observed.
What does the report consist of?	The report consists of symbols noting the occurrence of behaviors, or a numerical rating of behaviors, or answers to a set of questions about behaviors.

Procedure 2 Anecdotal Records (Semi-Structured)	Procedure 3 Observation by Experts (Unstructured)
The observer should be someone well trained in observing and describing behavior.	In addition to being an experienced observer, this person should be an expert in an area relevant to the program.
The behavior to be observed is broadly defined by the evaluator. The observer selects the relevant behavior based on the evaluator's broad guidelines.	The behavior to be observed is *not* defined by the evaluator. It is left entirely to the discretion of the observer.
The evaluator and observer together make these decisions or the evaluator makes them alone.	The evaluator and observer together make these decisions.
The observer records continuously during the session. The observer is told to observe and record either the behavior of specific individuals or specified activities, events, or social interactions (e.g., students tutoring one another).	The observer may take notes during the observation session, but the bulk of the report is written after the observation.
The report consists of anecdotal accounts. The behavior is described sequentially and nonjudgmentally. The observer may offer an interpretation or judgment at the end of the anecdotal description.	The report consists of a description of significant events and, if requested, judgments of the quality of the program activities (e.g., instruction or learning). The focus is frequently on social factors (i.e., how the people within the groups function with one another), although the observer is likely to comment on patterns of behavior of people who are working or playing alone if it seems that these patterns are significant.

puting the correlation coefficient between the results of both observers' records of the same event. A high correlation indicates substantial agreement between the two observers.

3. Procedure 1 yields quantitative data. Your evaluation report may be more persuasive if you have quantitative information to support your conclusions.

If you decide to use Procedure 1, there are three types of instruments that might be useful for your purposes: on-the-spot checklists, coded behavior records, and delayed report instruments.

On-the-spot checklists can be used for recording the presence, absence, or frequency of a few behaviors as they occur. Generally, a checklist does not tell you about the duration of the behaviors nor about the quality or intensity of the behaviors because of the need to control the length of the instrument. A long checklist is impossible to work with when a person is attempting to record on-the-spot behaviors.

Let us say that you have selected the following list of helping behaviors as the ones you will ask the observers to look for:

1. *Verbally volunteers to help another child*
2. *Explains a situation or assignment to the other child*
3. *Oversees the work of the other child*
4. *Loans materials to the other child*
5. *Hands the other child materials or objects related to the classwork*
6. *Praises the other child*
7. *Communicates to a third person the needs of the other child*
8. *Verbally encourages the other child*

These behaviors could be incorporated into an instrument to determine if they occur and/or how frequently they occur within a given time period. As you examine the list, however, you notice that it will not differentiate among various examples of behavior that fall within a given category. For example, one child saying to another, "No, you don't do it that way, you do it this way," would fall into category 2 listed above, regardless of whether the words are spoken neutrally or harshly. A *checklist* that could make these discriminations would probably be lengthy and therefore impractical.

Coded behavior records,[1] unlike checklists, enable you to record *in sequence* quite a few behaviors as they occur within a given time period. As with a checklist, the behaviors to be observed are preselected. They are translated into a workable code system which is taught to the observers. Here is an example of a relatively simple code system:

Basic Code:

A — teacher

B — helper

C — child being helped

r — requests

a — assigns

v — volunteers

p — praises

h — helps

Combination of Symbols:

Arv —teacher requests volunteers

AaBC —teacher assigns one child to help another

ApB —teacher praises helper

ApC —teacher praises child being helped

BpC —helper praises child she is helping

Bv —child volunteers to help another child

Bh —child engages in helping behaviors

BrA —helper requests help from teacher

Cr —child requests help

A coded behavior record can be a useful documentation tool. It can tell you whether prescribed activity sequences or patterns of personal interchange were carried out, and it can detect unanticipated interactions.

A major limitation of the coded behavior record is that it involves a lengthy and sometimes complicated procedure. Observers must be trained in the use of the code symbols; and once the information is gathered, the symbols must be decoded and interpreted. In addition, coded behavior records carry as a liability the potential that observers will miss critical events while recording. For this reason, they are mainly used for constructing transcriptions of events that have been filmed or videotaped. Films can be viewed several times to ensure accuracy and/or to measure the observer's reliability.

Delayed report instruments of one kind or another are the most commonly used classroom observation tools. One characteristic that distinguishes them from the other two techniques is that they are filled in immediately *after* the observation period. The amount of subjective interpretation required of the observer will vary according to the wording, but in general, most delayed report instruments require some inference or judgment. Delayed report instruments can be constructed using various formats. The following examples of items from delayed report instruments should suggest the range of possibilities.

Examples

Place a check anywhere on the horizontal line to
describe the behaviors you saw during tutoring:

|———————————————+———————————————|

Tutor persisted	Tutor explained	Tutor gave up
in explaining	two or three	immediately if
and demonstrating	times, but gave	child failed to
even though child	up after that	understand.
failed to under-	if child failed	
stand.	to understand.	

|———————————————+———————————————|

Tutor made	Tutor praised	Tutor didn't
encouraging state-	and encouraged	acknowledge suc-
ments; found some-	occasionally,	cess of child or
thing to praise	but missed some	else focussed on
even when child	obvious oppor-	failures; offered
did not fully	tunities to	little or no en-
understand.	praise and en-	couragement.
	courage.	

|———————————————+———————————————|

Tutor was involved	Tutor was in-	Tutor was not in-
in the task;	volved in task,	volved in the
focussed entire	but was some-	task; paid little
attention on	times distracted	attention to the
child.	by other class-	child.
	room events.	

Answer yes or no for each question concerning the process
you observed for selecting tutors.

yes   no

[ ]   [ ]   1) Did the teacher assign one child to work
            with another child?

[ ]   [ ]   2) Did children volunteer to work with one
            another without being asked?

[ ]   [ ]   3) Did some of the children who were asked to
            help another child resist or refuse to do
            so?

Check the statements that describe what occurred during
the course of the observation.

[ ] The groups formed *without* assistance from the teacher.

[ ] The plans for the day's activities were discussed
    before the students began to work on individual
    projects.

[ ] The groups were *not* dominated by single individuals.

Rate the quality of the group interaction you observed using the scale provided.

1 - unsatisfactory
2 - poor
3 - so-so
4 - good
5 - outstanding

1 2 3 4 5 A. The harmony with which the working group functioned.

1 2 3 4 5 B. The involvement of all members in contributing to group planning.

1 2 3 4 5 C. The willingness of the group to proceed without teacher assistance.

Place an "X" in the box indicating how often you observed each of the following activities:

	always	fre-quently	some-times	seldom	never
Did the teacher encourage students to work with one another?					
Did the teacher assign students to work together?					
Did the students form their own working groups?					

Procedures 2 and 3 for conducting observations, described in Table 3, are appropriate when you *cannot* define or describe the precise behaviors you are looking for. Because Procedures 2 and 3 involve a great degree of subjective judgment, the reliability or consistency with which these judgments are made will be open to challenge, and their credibility will depend ultimately on the ability and reputation of the observers you select.

Step 2 has presented alternatives for designing an observation system. Once you have chosen a method that meets your needs, you can proceed with the design of your observation plan.

Step 3. Select and prepare the observers and, if you are using an observation instrument, develop it.

If you are using Procedures 2 or 3 (semi-structured and unstructured procedures), the selection of observers is very important. You need people who have had sufficient experience in the classroom, work place, or other program arena to be able to identify the relevant events. A classroom, for example, is a complex environment, especially a classroom in which a fair amount of mobility is allowed the student. It often takes experienced observers to make sense of classroom events.

Whether you use master teachers, experienced supervisors, or professional evaluators as observers, take care that they have no bias which could affect their credibility. For example, you should think twice about asking someone with only structured-classroom teaching experience to be an observer in an unstructured classroom. And you would obviously not select anyone who has a stake in the success or failure of the program. Your choice of observers must still any suspicions that what is unexpected or undesired may go unnoticed or underemphasized; the ability of your observers to see what goes on and to accurately describe or categorize what they see is of paramount importance. And with Procedure 3, the persuasiveness of the information depends heavily upon the expertise and reputation of the observers.

In preparing observers for Procedures 2 and 3, think ahead to the time when you will be interpreting the information they provide. How might the information be organized to help you process it efficiently? It would probably be helpful to give the observers specific instructions about how you want the information conveyed.

Example of instructions given to a Procedure 2 observer

We would like the report to consist of two sections. In the first section, please prepare 20 anecdotal reports of the important incidents. By anecdotal reports, we mean verbal accounts that exhibit these characteristics:

1. Each anecdote should be limited to a single incident.
2. It should contain a factual, non-inferential description of the behaviors that characterize the incident. (For example, "She said, 'I don't want to be the big bad wolf!'" rather than, "She was unhappy with the part assigned her in the play.")
3. It should contain a description of the situation in which the behavior occurs so that the meaning of the behavior can be understood.
4. It should be written as soon as possible after the occurrence of the incident so that all important details are included.

In the second section, please assess and evaluate what you have seen during the observation. We are also interested in your judgments about the quality of what took place.

Another concern in preparing observers, regardless of whether you use Procedures 1, 2, or 3, is that you withhold certain kinds of information they *should not* know—information that is likely to prejudice their observations. For example, if observers are asked to cover several classrooms, some of which are program classrooms and some of which are not, you guard against bias by not telling them which is which.

If you are using Procedure 1, the highly structured procedure, the observers need only be disinterested and capable of learning to use the instrument you devise for the observation. Your purpose is to acquire a representative sample of behavior for your observers to witness, so you may want to train more observers than you think you will need in case some observers should for any reason be unable to fulfill their commitments. In general, the more evidence you expect to obtain from observation reports about the affective aspects of the program, the more observers you may require. When you choose Procedure 1, you should compare simultaneous tryout observations by your observers in pairs or, if possible, with a videotape of sample classroom behavior. Such a comparison is needed to show that the instrument works and that it is *reliable*—the observers using it produce similar and consistent results when observing the same situation.

Preparing observers to use a Procedure 1 instrument (on-the-spot checklists, coded behavior records, delayed report methods) requires that you or the work place and work with them until they understand, to your satisfaction, the relationship between the instrument items and the observed behaviors. This activity is critical. As has been said, even highly structured instruments demand some degree of inference and interpretation. *You will have to train your observers to infer the same things from the same behaviors.* Discuss the items with them, and have them make up hypothetical incidents and agree on how they would record them.

If you are using an instrument calling for the rating of behaviors, you should be alert to certain *rating error tendencies.* Many people tend to use only a limited number of options on a rating scale. Some give every item a very high rating (the generosity error), some give a very low rating (the severity error), and some give an average rating (the central tendency error). To guard against these personal response style errors, you should describe a set of behaviors covering the range of possible ratings and, if possible, point out such behaviors in a natural setting. You should also require that the observers engage in some supervised trial observations as part of their training.

Another common observer error is known as the *halo effect.* This occurs when an observer's *general* impression of a person biases his ratings of all the items or questions pertaining to that person's behavior. This type of error will become less likely—but will not be eliminated—if the observers remain unacquainted with the people they are observing. Nevertheless, you should work with all observers to ensure that they know about the dangers of halo effect and can make the appropriate distinctions called for in the instrument.

Regardless of which kind of instrument you decide to use, a good way to begin its development is to write out a short dramatization, in outline form, of the behaviors that participants would display if the program's objectives have been achieved. Say to yourself:

If I walked into the room in which these objectives had been achieved, this is what I would be likely to see. . . .

Then write out an alternate scenario—one describing behaviors that should *not* be seen if the objectives have been achieved. It will be equally persuasive in your final report to point to the *absence* of certain undesired behaviors as it is to point to the *presence* of desired ones. Some objectives, in fact, are most clearly stated in terms of the reduction of certain kinds of behavior (e.g., the objective of reducing the name-calling behavior of students in the classroom).

These two scenarios should provide you with the basis from which to construct the instrument. If you feel that you cannot write such scenarios because of lack of information, talk to program planners, visit programs, and seek information from people involved in implementing the program. Visiting the programs will give you a good perspective on what your observers are likely to encounter. If you feel you cannot write these scenarios because you think that the relevant behaviors cannot be described, then you should seriously reconsider your choice of Procedure 1.

The following lists provide an example of the range of possible subjects and behaviors to be considered in scenarios of the classroom helping behavior objective described at the beginning of this chapter.

Possible subjects of observations

1. Teacher only
2. Teacher interacting with whole group
3. Teacher interacting with individual students
4. Teacher interacting with small group
5. Individual students only
6. Two or more students interacting with one another

Possible categories of behavior

In constructing the instrument, you may wish to focus on one or more of the following aspects of the verbal or non-verbal behavior to be observed:

1. Its occurrence (Does it occur?)

2. Its frequency (How often does it occur?)
3. Its duration (How long does it last?)
4. Its quality (How intense, concerned, effective, etc., is it?)

Student behaviors

1. Play behaviors
2. Behaviors related to use of program materials
3. Attentive-inattentive behaviors
4. Caretaking behaviors related to self and others
5. Qualities of interaction (or non-interaction) with other students or teachers, such as assertive, affectionate, hostile, withdrawn
6. Types of vocal expression, such as praising, asking, telling, shouting, explaining.

Teacher behaviors

1. Nonverbal aspects of interactions with students: amount of smiling, shouting, number and type of interactions, instances of patting, touching, or other physical interaction
2. Statements or questions directed toward students: comments related to classroom management, positive or reinforcing comments, negative comments, categories of questions
3. Teacher movement in the classroom: amount of time spent in one section of the room, amount of time spent standing in one place, number of students contacted physically or verbally in a particular time period
4. Behaviors involving initiation of activities

The next step is to translate these scenarios into an instrument that defines the behaviors to be observed.[2] Constructing a suitable observation instrument will involve you in the decisions and precautions outlined below.

Suggestions for on-the-spot checklists

1. Keep the item number down, preferably below ten.
2. Place the items in some kind of logical sequence.
3. Check the wording of each item, and eliminate inferential words that are likely to be interpreted differently by different observers.
4. Decide on the way that information will be recorded. You may simply want to know if the behavior occurred *at all,* and thus a single check to note the occurrence would be sufficient:

☐   1) engaged in fighting behavior (pushed, hit, kicked, etc.)

☐   2) used racial slur

☐   3) destroyed school property (tore pages of textbook, carved name on desk, etc.)

On the other hand, you may want to know how frequently the behavior occurred, in which case you would ask the observer to tally the number of times that the behavior occurred:

_____   1) engaged in fighting behavior

_____   2) used racial slur

In either event, plan in advance how you will analyze, summarize, and report the information you obtain. Consult Chapter 12 about methods of data summarization before you produce the final draft of the observation instrument.

Suggestions for coded behavior records

1. Devise a manageable code, one in which the symbols can be easily learned by the observer. Obviously, this means that the number of symbols must be restricted, but combinations of symbols, where possible, can increase the repertoire of possible behavior descriptions.
2. Modify the instrument to clarify the information obtained as your needs require. For example, if the people being observed are likely to engage in the same behavior for a period of time, you may want to build into the instrument a means of distinguishing between behavior of long duration and behavior of short duration.
3. Design the recording sheets with an eye to the time when the information is to be decoded and interpreted. If the job of decoding can be done by a clerk or aide, you will save yourself much time. Again, early attention to precisely how information will be analyzed and reported, discussed in Chapter 12, will prevent waste in effort spent collecting unnecessary or uninterpretable information.

Suggestions for delayed report instruments

1. After you decide on a format (questionnaire, rating sheet, checklist) and write your items, check the wording of each question or item to see if you can reduce the level of inference and still obtain the information you need. Eliminate words that are likely to be interpreted differently by different observers.

2. In deciding on the observation time unit, keep in mind that the longer the delay between the observation and completion of the instrument, the less dependable the rating. You may narrow the time gap by requesting that the observers switch from observation to recording two or more times *within* the total observation time. If you adopt such a procedure, you may also want to modify the layout of your recording sheets to reflect this division of observation time:

	Observa- tion #1	Observa- tion #2	Observa- tion #3
To what extent does the working group function harmoniously?	1-2-3-4-5	1-2-3-4-5	1-2-3-4-5

3. Before you design the final draft of the instrument, consult Chapter 12 and plan how you will analyze and report results of the observation.

Step 4. Decide on who will be observed and when.

Not all individuals and all activities can be observed. Consequently, you must select the subjects of the observations, the number of observations, and when they are to occur.

1. Are you going to preselect the subjects and provide the observers with the names of specific people, or are you going to ask the observer to make on-the-spot selections based on who is engaging in a particular activity?
2. Will the observer stay with one person or group for an entire observation period, or will the subjects change during that period?
3. How many observations will provide convincing evidence that the findings represent recurring behavior?
4. At what points during the program should these observations take place?
5. What is the optimum time of day for the observation: the beginning of the day? mid-morning? Check the daily activities schedule before deciding.
6. How much time should the observer spend at the location for any given observation period?

Step 5. Make the necessary arrangements.

After deciding on the desired agenda for observations, you must finalize the plans and provide for the acceptance of the observers at the site where they will observe.

1. Inform and instruct the observers. Answer any last-minute questions, and see to the practical needs, such as travel arrangements.
2. Inform other interested parties such as administrators, supervisors, or teachers. A teacher's expectation of being observed on a given day may influence what happens in class on that day, so in order to increase the likelihood that *typical* behavior will be observed, you can arrange it so that the teachers know that an observer (or more than one observer) is coming, but do not know the specific day. Tell teachers or others about the purpose of the observation in order to minimize their anxiety.

When the observations have been made and the data recorded and gathered, you will face the task of summarizing it and interpreting the results for your report. Chapter 12 offers some guidance.

Notes

1. For a more detailed explanation of how and when to use this type of instrument, see *How to Assess Program Implementation*, Volume 5 of the *Program Evaluation Kit*.
2. If you are planning to computerize the resulting data, be sure to consult someone who is knowledgeable about the computer that is available to you. The structure of your instrument can be crucially affected by the information this person can provide.

For Further Reading

King, J. A., Morris, L. L., & Fitz-Gibbon, C. T. (1987). *How to assess program implementation.* Newbury Park, CA: Sage. If you are interested in determining whether classroom practices conform to a program's instructional guidelines, this book will be useful. Part of the *Program Evaluation Kit*, it contains a section on developing observation schedules for that purpose.

Chapter 10
Developing Your Own Measures: Sociometric Instruments

The suggestions in this chapter for helping you to develop and use sociometric instruments are organized according to the following five steps:

1. Identify the program objective to be measured with sociometric instruments; determine what specific information you want.
2. Decide on the approach you will use.
3. Develop the instrument.
4. Administer the instrument.
5. Summarize and analyze the data.

Step 1. Identify the program objective to be measured with sociometric instruments; determine what specific information you want.

Consider the example of the evaluator who is attempting to determine the social and attitudinal outcomes of a bussing program in which a group of children from one school are integrated into six classrooms at another school:

Example

Program objective: By the end of the year, the children who have been bussed will feel comfortable and accepted in their new environment. Classroom friendship patterns will reflect their acceptance and integration into the new school.

Information to be obtained from a sociometric instrument:

1. Have classroom friendships developed between children who have been bussed and those who have not?
2. Are the classroom social groups such that the bussed children have formed groups separate from the other children?
3. Have any of the children who have been bussed assumed positions of leadership in the classroom?
4. Have any of the children who have been bussed become generally popular?
5. Who are the social isolates in the class? Do the children who have been bussed fall into this category out of proportion to their numbers?

Step 2. Decide on the approach you will use.

There are two approaches to the construction of sociometric measures. Respondents can be asked to *rate their peers* or to *make choices* from a set of reality-oriented social options. You may wish to use one or the other, or some combination of these two approaches.

The following items might be found on a *peer-rating* instrument:

- *Someone at work is nice to everyone and has lots of friends. Who is it?*
- *Someone in class has good ideas and thinks of fun things to do. Who is it?*
- *Here is someone at work who offers to help when someone needs help.*
- *Here is someone in class who is often chosen by the kids to be captain of a team.*
- *Name someone who you think would do a good job of representing your class on the school council.*
- *Name someone who would do a good job of organizing an office party.*

Peer-rating items such as these can be used to discover which children are perceived by the others as being popular, and which ones are seen as the leaders in general.

The other approach is to ask people to list their own choices of companions for various activities from among their co-workers or classmates. This is the method of *social choice.* The following items are examples:

- *I would like to work with the following people.*
- *I would like to sit at the same table with the following people.*
- *I would like to be in a group for leisure activities with the following people.*

Social-choice items focus on social *preferences,* and should be distinguished from items such as the following, which describe existing social situations:

- *I now spend most of my time in class working with the following classmates.*
- *I now spend most of my play time with the following classmates.*

Although responses to these two types of items could overlap, there might be differences as well. Children and adults find themselves in social situations for a variety of reasons, some of which have little to do with social preferences. An obvious example is one in which a child plays most frequently with another child because the two are next-door neighbors. In class, they prefer other play companions. There may, of course, be some situation in which you want to know about *discrepancies* between preferences and existing situations. If such information is not of concern, use social-preference items, since the responses to the other type of item can present interpretation problems.

Both peer-rating and social-choice instruments are easy to administer and interpret. Social-choice instruments provide information on friendship patterns, while peer-rating instruments identify leaders.

Step 3. Develop the instrument.

In constructing your sociometric measure, keep in mind the list of questions that the instrument is supposed to address, produced in Step 1. In addition, the following guidelines are worth noting:

1. *In constructing social-choice instruments, make the choice options general rather than specific.* Mention general activities (work with, play with, sit next to) rather than specific ones (walk to the school assembly with) when asking people to list choices of companions. You should also avoid goal-oriented choices (paint a picture with, be on the same team with), since these reflect people's assessment of one another's competencies.

   It is important that items be phrased so that the choice options include everyone and are available to everyone in the group. For example, if some students go home for lunch, you should not include an item such as this:

   I would like to sit next to _____*in the cafeteria.*

2. *Avoid negative items.* Negative items are statements or questions like these:

   - *If there are people that you don't want to work with, place their names here.*
   - *Whom would you least like to sit next to?*
   - *Here is someone who doesn't seem to have many friends in class.*

   Although they may clearly identify persons who have been rejected by the group, negative items can undermine morale or do injury to individuals who would be singled out. Since they also fail to throw light on why certain individuals are rejected, the losses involved in using negative sociometric items outweigh the possible gains.

3. *The number of responses requested for each item depends on your choice of item type and the age of the individuals.* If you decide on a peer rating instrument, there is no reason to limit the number of names that may be provided for each item. You may even wish to encourage the respondent to list as many names per item as seem appropriate.

When you use a social choice approach, however, it is advisable to call for about *five choices* from adults or from children in the upper elementary grades and *three choices* from children in the lower elementary grades. The three choice format will be necessary to fit the younger child's limited ability to deal with hypothetical questions; whereas five choices will yield stable information, taking into account the daily fluctuations in people's friendship patterns. What's more, five choices will keep you from arriving at erroneous conclusions. Consider the bussing example in which children have been asked to provide the names of *five* classmates with whom they wish to associate. If they fail to include the names of any bussed children, you have strong evidence that the objective has *not* been achieved—a conclusion you could not defend if each child had been asked to provide the names of only one or two classmates.

Step 4. Administer the instrument.

Depending on the age of the individuals, instructions can be given orally or they can be written. Instructions should include the following information:

- The number of names that should be listed in response to any one item, and whether the option exists of providing fewer names than called for
- Whether certain items can be skipped
- Whether one person's name can be used as a response to more than one item
- Whether the respondent must indicate the last names of those chosen, or the initials of the last names, or whether the first names are sufficient for some choices.

The person who administers the instrument should be someone the participants know and feel they can trust, such as a classroom teacher or personnel director. Furthermore, it is important to assure the participants that their responses will be kept confidential.

The following is adapted from a sociometric instrument developed by Norman E. Gronlund (1959). Notice that the choices are reality-oriented.

Name_____ Date_____

Please fill in the blanks.

· Your choices must be from students in this room, including those who are absent.
· You should give the first name and the initial of the last name.
· You should make all five choices for each question.
· You may choose a student for more than one group if you wish.
· Your choices will not be seen by anyone else.

I would choose to *sit near* these classmates:
1. _____ 4. _____
2. _____ 5. _____
3. _____

I would choose to *work with* these classmates:
1. _____ 4. _____
2. _____ 5. _____
3. _____

I would choose to *play with* these classmates:
1. _____ 4. _____
2. _____ 5. _____
3. _____

Step 5. Summarize and analyze the data.

If you have used a peer rating instrument (e.g., "_____ is someone who is nice to everyone."), tallying the results simply requires that you count the number of times each person was named:

Arlene Adams	卌 卌 卌 ‖
Brian Berry	卌
Carol Cooper	‖‖
David Davis	卌 卌 ‖
Ellen Evans	‖‖

If you have used a social choice instrument (e.g., "Whom do you want to sit next to?"), you can either do a simple tally, as in the above example, or you can construct a matrix table (adapted from Gronlund, 1959) as in the example that follows. Such a table will tell you:

• Who chose whom
• Which choices were mutual

- Whether the choices were from one group or another (e.g., in the matrix below, data for boys and girls are displayed separately)

	Pupils choosing	Pupil #	1	2	3	4	5	6	7	8	OS	SS
Girls	Adams, Arlene	1	▓	(x)		x				x	1	2
	Cooper, Carol	2	(x)	▓		(x)					0	2
	Evans, Ellen	3		x	▓	(x)		x			1	2
	Lee, Linda	4		(x)	(x)	▓		(x)			1	2
Boys	Berry, Brian	5				x	▓	(x)	x		1	2
	Davis, David	6				(x)	(x)	▓	(x)		1	2
	Fink, Fred	7		x				(x)	▓		1	1
	Garden, Graham	8					x			▓	0	1
Choices received		OS	0	1	0	2	0	2	0	1		
		SS	1	3	1	3	2	2	2	0		
Mutual choices		OS	0	0	0	1	0	1	0	0		
		SS	1	2	1	2	1	2	1	0		

Column headers: **Pupils chosen** (1–8), **Choices given** (OS, SS)

SS = same sex   OS = opposite sex   Circled x's = mutual choices

This is how you would read the matrix:

Beginning with Arlene Adams (Pupil #1), we see that she has chosen Carol Cooper (#2), Linda Lee (#4), and ·Graham Garden (#8). Carol Cooper (#2) has chosen Arlene Adams (#1) and Linda Lee (#4). When the choice is mutual, the X is circled. Thus we see that Arlene Adams and Carol Cooper chose one another, as did Carol Cooper and Linda Lee.

By listing first one group (girls) and then the other (boys), the matrix divides naturally into four rectangles. Boxes in the upper left display the *same* sex choices made by the girls, while those in the upper right show *opposite* sex choices made by the girls. Boxes in the lower left display *opposite* sex choices made by the boys, while those in the lower right show *same* sex choices made by the boys. Because the children on this kind of measure could not choose themselves, the cells occupying the self-choice positions have been blackened, indicating that such choices do not apply here.

For Further Reading

Gronlund, N. E. (1959). *Sociometry in the classroom.* New York: Harper & Brothers. This book provides a wealth of information on sociometric instruments and their uses in the classroom.

Chapter 11
Validity and Reliability
of Attitude Instruments

The following discussion attempts to pull together some ideas which were touched upon in the previous chapters. Its objective is to convey in relatively straightforward language the major issues in measurement that deal in one way or another with the notions of validity and reliability. It is hoped that this informal introduction to the subject will be useful to you, whether it helps you to interpret the manuals that accompany instruments you purchase, or guides you in determining the quality of instruments you construct yourself.

The major purpose of this chapter is instructional. To give you a concrete situation to which you can "pin" this new information, try to read with your own attitude instrument in mind. If the instrument you are using is, like an attitude rating scale, one which will yield a *single summary number* to indicate an individual's status with respect to a certain attitude as discussed in Chapter 6, then your instrument is like an achievement test, and you should find the discussion in this chapter easily applicable. This is because concepts of validity and reliability, as well as methods for assessing them, have evolved around achievement testing, where a *single number*, say, a percentile score, is used as an indicator of presence of a skill.

If your instrument is a questionnaire, interview, or a delayed report observation instrument,[1] to be interpreted and reported *question-by-question*, then you must prepare yourself for reading this chapter. In your situation, *each question* must be considered an *individual measure* of an attitude, an instrument in itself. If you think about your measurement situation, you will notice that this is indeed the case. If you are designing a questionnaire to measure management's attitudes about in-service training of employees, for instance, it might contain questions such as the following: (1) "To what extent do you feel in-service training has affected the quality of performance in your company?" (2) "Would you be willing to offer increased numbers of in-service hours to employees?" You might intend that answers to these questions be scored and reported independently. If you have assembled a questionnaire of this sort, you actually have a choice of *two* approaches to reporting results, and subsequently to assessment of validity and reliability:

1. You may consider each of your questions an independent measure of a separate attitude. In this case, read the chapter accordingly, substituting for yourself the word "question" every time "measure" appears in the text.

2. You might consider *combining* the results of several questions on your questionnaire or interview to form an *index* of an attitude. Calculating an index generally increases the reliability and validity of the instrument by providing multiple samples from the same attitude within a single instrument. If you are interested in constructing a measure in this way, you are encouraged to do so and should include in your instrument three or four questions aimed at essentially the same attitude. Should you decide to include indices of this sort in your questionnaire, interview, or delayed report observation measure, then read the chapter substituting the word "index" for "measure."

Measurement: Validity and Reliability

Assessments of validity and reliability help to determine the amount of faith people should place in a measurement instrument. "Validity" and "reliability" refer to different aspects of a measure's believability. Judgments of *validity* answer the question: Is the instrument an appropriate one for what needs to be measured? And *reliability* indicators answer: Does the instrument yield consistent results? These are questions you must ask about any measure you select, whether you buy it or construct it yourself. It may be helpful to remember that "valid" has the same root as "valor" and "value" (and maybe even "valentine"), referring to strength or worth. Validity indicates how worthwhile a measure is likely to be, in a given situation, for telling you what you need to know. Validity boils down to whether the instrument is giving you the true story, or at least something approximating the truth.

"Reliability" when used to refer to tests carries the same meaning as when it refers to friends. A reliable friend is one on whom you can count to behave *the same way time and again.* A test, or questionnaire, or interview instrument that gives you essentially the same results when read-ministered is an instrument that is reliable in this sense.

Please note that reliability refers to consistency, but consistency does not guarantee truthfulness. A friend, for instance, who compliments your taste in clothes each time he sees you is certainly reliable but may not necessarily be telling the truth. What is more, he may not even be deliberately misleading you. It may be just a habit, or perhaps his judg-ment is skewed by an appreciation of your many other good features. Similarly, an instrument's being reliable does *not* mean that it is a good measure of what it seems to measure.

Consider a situation in which a one-question attitude instrument is used to monitor teachers' opinions about a new reading program. Four times during the school year they are asked, "Do you believe the XYZ Program is more effective than the old program in helping students learn to read?" All but one teacher answers "yes" every time, and a maverick always answers "no." The question is marvelously reliable. It gets the same answer each time. The reliability of the question is no proof that the answers given reflect the teachers' true feelings. You may, in fact, hear consider-able lunchroom grumbling that shows widespread periodic displeasure with the program. The message of this discussion is that *a reliable measure is not necessarily valid.*

Is a valid measure reliable? In general, yes. A valid instrument is one that has demonstrated that it detects some "real" ability, attitude, or prevailing situation that the test user can identify and characterize. *If the ability or attitude is itself stable,* and if a respondent's answers to the items are not affected by other unpredictable factors, then each administration of the instrument should yield essentially the same results.

A demonstration of reliability, therefore, is necessary but not conclu-sive evidence that an instrument is valid. All the reliability studies in the world will not guarantee validity. Bear this in mind particularly when reading about the technical adequacy of published tests. Since reliability is easier to demonstrate than validity, the technical manuals that accompany tests and published attitude instruments often report reliability data *only.* The publisher intends to imply validity through demonstrating reliability. This is poor practice and amounts to doing half the job. Administrators need more adequate information if they are to justify using the test for making important decisions.

Validity: Is the Instrument an Appropriate One to Measure What You Want to Know?

People invest time and effort in measurement for one of two reasons:

1. They want to detect *how much* of something—a skill, attitude, or

ability—a person or thing has. This is a *descriptive* function of measurement, and the one most relevant to program evaluation. Though the standard used to decide successful performance differs, both normed and objectives-based achievement tests attempt to assess how much knowledge or skill an individual has acquired. Attitude instruments, similarly, seek to detect the quantity of some attitude or affective trait possessed by the respondents.

2. They want to predict some other, possibly future, performance or state of the person or thing, usually for the purpose of making a specific decision. When a test serves a *predictive* function, the primary interest is in obtaining a sample of present behavior upon which to base an expectation about how a person will perform in another, more complex setting. This is the case with tests used for making decisions about placement in special programs.

When you use a test, attitude survey, or observation instrument, you want to rely on the measure to accomplish one of these two things. In either case, the instrument provides a sample of behavior that supports conclusions about performance in a broader, real-life context. The validity of an instrument reflects the sureness with which you can draw such conclusions.

In fact, it will serve you well to think of validity as *the extent to which you can rule out interpretations of the instrument's results other than the one you wish to make.* Establishing an instrument's validity requires that you anticipate the potential arguments that skeptics might use to dismiss your results. When measuring attitudes with self-report instruments such as questionnaires, for instance, the most frequent argument of the skeptic goes like this:

> *Respondents have an idea of which answers are socially desirable. Not wishing to appear deviant, they hide their true feelings and bend their answers to conform to a model of how they ought to answer.*

Where this happens, the instrument is of course not measuring true attitudes; rather, it is detecting people's ideas about what is socially acceptable. Such an instrument is invalid and useless. The wise questionnaire developer will find a way to demonstrate that social desirability minimally affects answers. This can be done in several ways. One way is to show that the questionnaire actually predicts some future or concurrent behavior of respondents. It might, for instance, differentiate frequent meeting attenders from non-attenders. Or the instrument might be constructed in such a way (by making responses anonymous, for instance) that an argument can be made to dismiss charges of bias.

The credibility of your evaluation will be profoundly affected by the perceived validity of your measures. For this reason, you should include an assessment, even if informal, of each instrument's validity in your evaluation report. *Four major approaches* to determining if an instrument is valid have evolved during the history of testing. Each represents a different aspect of the problem of building a case for the appropriateness of a test for a given situation. Three of the approaches have derived from using measurement instruments for description—determining how much skill or attitude people have. The fourth approach focuses on the usefulness of a measure as a predictor of some future behavior.

Approach 1: Descriptive Use of an Instrument: Construct Validity

The word "construct" is a handy one for discussing measurement instruments. It is a catch-all term used to refer to the skill, attitude, or ability that an instrument is intended to measure. "Ability to add decimals," "job satisfaction," "need for achievement," and "spatial ability" are all constructs. *The construct validity of an instrument is the extent to which you can be sure it represents the construct whose name appears in its title.* A test with good construct validity can be considered a substitute for actually observing a person displaying a skill or attitude in everyday life.

To adequately defend the construct validity of a test, other explanations for what the test measures must be satisfactorily ruled out. The ease of demonstrating construct validity for a particular instrument depends largely on the specificity of the construct itself. Sometimes the construct to be measured will be one for which test items seem clearly to represent the construct being measured. Such is the case with the ability to multiply fractions, answer questions about bonds in organic chemistry, take shorthand dictation, or report whether you would like to serve as a volunteer fund raiser. In these cases, people generally agree on what the construct looks like, so defending the instrument's validity simply involves describing how the instrument was developed and administered, and comparing it with similar published instruments if such exist.

Often, particulary in *attitude* measurement, the construct will be "fuzzy," imprecise, or complex as in the case of "self-esteem," "attitude toward school," or "teacher warmth." No clear, widely accepted definitions yet exist for these. In such cases, demonstrating construct validity will demand a preliminary step—precise construct definition.

Construct definition. Before you consider the validity of the measurement instrument (actually, before you write or select the instrument), you will have to define the construct as precisely as possible.[2] Defining the construct means explaining what you mean by, say, "self-esteem" or "need for achievement" and pointing out how your definition might differ from those given by others. The definition should also include some or all of the following:

1. A list or graph (see Figure 5, p. 140) of its distinctive features, possibly based on previous writing about the construct, including its subcomponents and their relationships to one another. This should include a description of how a person with a lot or a little of the construct might behave.

2. A list of closely related constructs with which your construct might be confused, and an argument about why your construct is distinct from those.

Composing this general description will help you justify that the skill or attitude you are attempting to measure is a real factor influencing behavior. You will have to anticipate and answer arguments to the contrary, for example, that the behaviors you say come from "self-esteem," are actually better described as "self-control," or that self-esteem is not a stable construct, but results, rather, in different behaviors in different people.

Once construct definition has been satisfactorily accomplished, you still must show that the *instrument itself* is valid. This means showing how the instrument overcomes extraneous sources of bias, such as ability to "psych out" a questionnaire and give only desirable answers, or a wish to hide one's true feelings.

Defending construct validity. Having written an extensive description of the construct to be measured, the validity of your instrument can be supported in several ways.

1. *Opinions of judges.* Let us say that you have prepared a questionnaire attempting to determine teachers' attitudes toward individualized instruction. You can get some idea of the validity of the questionnaire by showing it to a group of judges—perhaps curriculum specialists or teachers—without telling them its purpose. If the judges' individual conclusions about what the instrument seems to be measuring closely agree, then you have some evidence of construct validity. In this instance, each judge would have to notice that the test seemed to assess teacher attitudes about individualized classroom activities and individual pacing of students. The judges would also have to agree that results were unlikely to be affected by the teachers' desire to please or to hide their true feelings.

   Using the opinions of judges to assess an instrument's validity, you should be warned, will produce credible results to the extent that your judges merit the trust of the audience. If the judges themselves lack qualifications, or if they stand to benefit from instrument bias, then their judgments will be vulnerable to challenge.

2. *Correlations.*[3] Another measure of the same or a related construct can be administered to a group of people and then correlated with results from your instrument for these same people to yield evidence about validity. You might, for instance, be able to show that your measure of

"self-esteem" correlates positively with indicators of emotional health such as teacher or supervisor ratings of confidence, sociability, or leadership; or negatively with detectors of problems such as ratings of introversion or social isolation or even tardiness and truancy. You would also expect a positive, but perhaps moderate, correlation of the self-esteem measure with achievement.

You might also demonstrate that scores on the instrument *do not* correlate at all (that is, have correlations close to zero) with characteristics thought to be irrelevant to the one in question. You would expect, for instance, that a measure of self-esteem will be unrelated to manual dexterity or to age of respondents. A whole methodology using "Multitrait Multimethod Matrices" (see Campbell & Fiske, 1959) has evolved for estimating validity by means of a table of correlations with measures similar and different from the one in question.

3. *Criterion-group studies.* If possible, find a group of people judged to possess an abundance or deficiency of the construct in question and administer the instrument to them. Demonstrating that people judged independently to be high in self-esteem, for instance, score well on the instrument and that people judged low score low builds a strong case for the instrument's validity. Criterion group studies are always wise to perform, particularly if you are developing an instrument yourself. In addition to assessing validity, they help you to identify items that are inadequate for measuring the construct (or which give *unreliable* responses). Discarding these will improve the quality of the instrument by increasing both its validity and reliability.

If you cannot find a criterion group, you might try administering the instrument to a group of people who have been preinstructed to answer as if they possessed the construct to be measured. While the information this method yields will not be as credible as that obtained from a true criterion group, it will still provide a better instrument tryout than none at all.

4. *Appeal to logic.* Many times, particularly when the construct can be easily defined, audiences will accept the instrument as logically related to the construct as long as they know that it has been administered fairly, that is:

- Enough time has been allowed for its administration so that respondents are not rushed.
- Pressure to respond in a particular way is absent from the instrument's format and instructions, from the setting of its administration, and from the personal manner of the administrator.

In every measurement situation, you are asking not only that the audience accept the instrument's representation of the construct; you are also asking them to agree that the *circumstances of its administration* have not invalidated your results.

It should be apparent by now that demonstrating instrument validity is not an all-or-nothing matter. Actually, any combination of the types of evidence described here that you are able to assemble can be used as support for construct validity. If you plan to use an instrument more than once, consider the whole period of its use an opportunity to collect validity information. Each administration is a chance to collect information about the opinions of judges, its correlation with the respondents' performance on other measures, and the performance of criterion groups, as well as its concurrent and predictive validity, to be discussed below. Establishing construct validity should be a continuing process.

Approach 2. Descriptive Use of an Instrument: Content Validity

Before an instrument can be written to test for the presence of a particular skill, aptitude, or attitude, the construct has to be translated into a set of distinctive *behaviors*. The behaviors are described in terms of how people tend to act, or what people tend to say, or perhaps what others tend to say about them. A measurement instrument is constructed on the basis of such characteristic behaviors.

Now any complex construct, such as "attitude toward school," will be definable as several different types of behavior, and its accurate detection may even require using more than one kind of measurement instrument.

Figure 5, for example, shows a collage of the many behaviors that might collectively indicate positive attitude toward school.

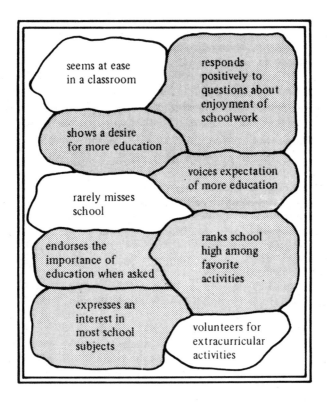

Figure 5. Collage of the behaviors hypothetically symptomatic of *positive attitude toward school.* Shaded behaviors will be assessed by means of an attitude rating scale. Sizes of pieces show relative importance of each set of behaviors to manifestation of the overall construct.

The shaded behavior categories in the figure lend themselves to assessment by means of an attitude rating scale *which will yield a single score;* the unshaded behaviors will require *other* measurement methods, principally examination of school records and classroom observations. The following discussion focuses on the content validity of the attitude rating scale only.

Examination of the shaded areas of Figure 5 will bring to mind any number of questions that could be written for inclusion in the attitude rating scale. A complete list of all possible relevant questions would constitute an immense collection. Since no questionnaire can hope to ask them all, the actual instrument must contain a *sample* of the possible questions. *Content validity refers to the representativeness of the sample of questions included in the instrument.*[4] This means that a questionnaire based on Figure 5's shaded sections would have to do two things. It must:

1. Contain questions that represent each of the six categories of behavior to be represented.

2. Give emphasis to each category according to the proportion it contributes to the construct as depicted in the figure. This can be controlled by means of the number of questions asked, or the number of points assigned to each question in scoring. In a questionnaire with high content validity, then, *"responds positively to questions about enjoyment of schoolwork"* would occupy roughly twice as many items (or each of its items would receive twice as many points toward the total score) as *"voices expectation of more education,"* though both would be represented.

High content validity means that the test "maps onto" the collection of possible questions by sampling representatively from its various manifestations as in Figure 6.

A measure that focuses too heavily on one category—as in Figure 7—is not content valid for measuring the whole. It is content valid only for the category it does measure. The attitude rating scale in Figure 7, for instance, could be more accurately named, "Questionnaire on Interest in School Subjects With a Little Work Enjoyment Thrown In."

Unfortunately, little is currently known about the psychological composition of complex skills and imprecise attitude constructs like attitude toward school, and there is a corresponding uncertainty about the various behaviors that reflect their existence. There is, of course, no neat photo of the psyche to serve as a basis for test construction. It is a difficult if not impossible task for researchers to confirm speculations about the subdivisions of constructs and their behavioral indicators. Because of this, test builders must either rely on hunches or use fairly technical analytical procedures to define the constructs they aim to assess.[5]

When you attempt to display content validity of your own instruments, the best thing to do is to provide assurance that you

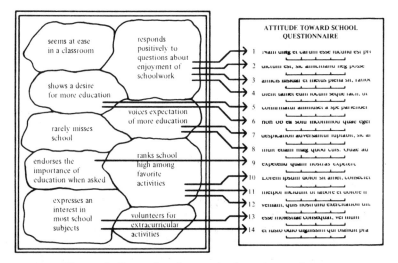

Figure 6. Example of an attitude rating scale questionnaire with *good* content validity. Each type of behavior representing the construct *attitude toward school* is adequately represented.

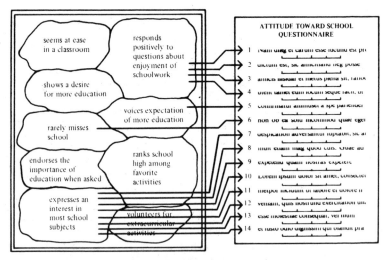

Figure 7. Example of an attitude rating scale questionnaire with *poor* content validity. Its questions too heavily represent some minor components of the construct *attitude toward school,* while other components are either weakly represented or totally ignored.

- Have not left out any important behaviors
- Have not included too much emphasis on a single sub-area of potential behaviors

Some attempt should be made to demonstrate construct and content validity whenever you discuss the use of an instrument that is intended to describe "how much" of a skill or attitude people possess. You will notice that neither form of validity is easy to determine. So far, no one has come up with a yardstick that leaves you with a number; you cannot report a "validity of .93" or that a particular interview instrument is "75% valid." The best way to describe a measure's validity in your report will be to consider possible challenges that might be made to its appropriateness for the particular situation, and to marshall the information you have assembled to answer each of them in turn.

Approach 3. Descriptive Use of a Test:
Concurrent Validity

The concurrent validity of an instrument is established by collecting data to see if the results obtained with the instrument agree with results from other instruments, administered at approximately the same time, to measure the same thing. Let us say, for example, that an attitude rating scale given to the students in the program demonstrated improved attitudes toward computers. At the same time, the program managers, in other reports, also said that employee attitudes toward computers were improving. The manager reports and the attitude rating scale would be, in effect, validating each other.

"When would anyone want to calculate concurrent validity?" you might wonder. It is useful in two situations:

1. Some circumstances call for a relatively *quick* estimate of the current state of a group's attitudes or abilities. Concurrent validity is often calculated on a measure that someone has developed in order to shorten the time spent testing. For instance, a questionnaire to students at the end of the term about the quality of laboratory instruction in a physics course might be considered as a substitute for the department chairperson's frequent visits if questionnaire results correlate favorably with information obtained from the visits.

2. Demonstrating concurrent validity of an instrument provides good evidence of its *construct* validity. If it gives you results similar to those from another instrument and that instrument's validity for measuring a particular construct has been fairly well established, then you can build a case that your instrument also measures the construct. This use of

correlational evidence to establish validity is discussed at the top of page 136.

Concurrent validity is determined by calculating a correlation coefficient between results from the instrument in question and results for the same individuals on a different measure of similar or related behavior, where both sets of results are taken to represent the status of the individuals during the same period of time. This correlation statistic is then recorded and discussed in the evaluation report. (Setting up data for calculating a correlation coefficient is briefly discussed on page 150.

Approach 4. Decision-Related Use of a Test: Predictive Validity

As already described, construct, content, and concurrent validity are concerned with how well an instrument represents a person's possession of a certain construct—a skill, attitude, or ability. It often happens that test developers care little about exactly *what* a test measures, preferring to define its value in terms of its ability to *predict future behavior*. For these situations, developers have employed methods for determining predictive validity.

The predictive validity of an instrument is established by demonstrating that the results from the instrument can be used to predict some future behavior. For example, if students who reported a liking for math on a questionnaire later signed up for math labs in larger numbers than students who reported not liking math, one could say that the questionnaire was in fact distinguishing between those who do and do not like math, and might be used with comparable accuracy to make similar predictions. Predictive, like concurrent, validity can be calculated and expressed as a correlation coefficient relating the instrument in question to a valid measure of the later-occurring predicted behavior.

In the best of all possible worlds, each applicable kind of validity would be assessed each time an instrument is constructed. Rarely is the validity question so thoroughly attacked, however. You will have to be the judge of how much time and effort you can devote to establishing the validity of the instruments you employ. Your evaluation report should frankly note validity problems that have had to be left unresolved.

Threats to Validity

The following are reasons why efforts to make valid measurements of attitudes frequently fail:

1. *The inevitably weak link between attitudes and behavior.* People attempt to measure attitudes because they sense a strong connection between attitudes and behavior. Yet so far results have been disappointing: attitude instruments generally have little predictive validity. Experience has shown that, say, students who report a liking for math frequently do not elect to participate in math labs. The problem may be that the attitude measured is only one of many factors contributing to the behavior. Perhaps those students do in fact like math, but they like music appreciation, the alternative activity during the math lab period, even better. Or perhaps they choose activities on the basis of being with their friends rather than on the basis of their academic interests.

   In summary, all other things being equal, attitudes might predict behavior, but since other things are rarely equal, the relationship between attitude and behavior is often weak.

2. *Response bias* due to desire to please, or *evaluation apprehension.* Responses to attitude measures may not be entirely frank because of the respondents' fears that they will be judged negatively or will be exposed to criticism. This will be especially true in cases where the possible responses to an issue vary in their social desirability. For example, asking parent employees if they have problems with child care may elicit "NO" responses, despite problems, if these workers think they should appear to have everything under control and that they should not let personal problems affect their work.

3. *Lack of comprehension or self-awareness.* People cannot respond accurately to questions they do not understand. Sometimes, too, a question may appear to be understood, but the person may not be aware of his or her own attitudes. Young children, for example, may not be sufficiently introspective to know their attitudes, and adults may unconsciously avoid recognizing certain attitudes in themselves.

4. *Lack of objectivity in administration.* In cases where reports of others are used, it is important to consider the extent to which the "others," those who are reporting the attitudes or behaviors, may be biased. Perhaps they themselves have something to gain from responding in a particular way.

   One kind of bias from others which threatens the credibility of an evaluation arises when the reporters provide data for comparisons between experimental and control groups. If the reporters know which group is the experimental group, they may, even unconsciously, be more generous to one or another of the groups, depending on their expectations. The only way to guard against such bias (if possible!) is to keep reporters unaware of the results you are hoping to find. Reporters should not know what results are expected from any group they are observing. This is called keeping them "blind."

For example, suppose a program aims to improve students' adjustment to school. A school psychologist interviews a sample of students to examine their adjustment to school; the sample includes students from the program and students from the control group (not in the program). The psychologist should not know which students are or are not in the program, since this could unfairly influence the interview results; and even if this prior knowledge did not in fact influence the psychologist's findings, it might be hard to convince people of that. Similarly, if observers are reporting observations of several experimental classrooms and of a group of control classrooms, the observers should not, if possible, be aware of which classrooms are E-group rooms and which are C-group rooms.

5. *Too few items.* Often attitude instruments rely on a single question to detect the presence or extent of an attitude. A single item is open to myriad errors of interpretation and formulation of a response. The skeptic can always challenge results from a single item on the grounds of indeterminate effects from both random and purposeful errors.

Summary

Remember that validity has to do with an instrument's appropriateness for accomplishing your purposes. These purposes might be to describe people or make a decision about them, or both. If you wish to describe them, you want to discuss how much of some attitude, skill, or ability (construct) they have. If you expect your audience to accept the results from an instrument used for this purpose, you demonstrate construct, content, or concurrent validity, and preferably all three. Construct validity refers to how well the instrument measures what it claims to. Demonstrating construct validity demands clear definition of the construct, then presentation of logical arguments, credible opinions, and evidence from correlational or criterion-group studies—all aimed at ruling out alternative explanations of the instrument's results. Content validity refers to how well the items give appropriate emphasis to the various components of the construct. To show content validity, you should provide evidence that the instrument contains a set of items that sample the construct's various sub-areas and that give each its proportionate emphasis. Concurrent validity is calculated when you use the results of one measure to predict the results of an alternative contemporaneous measure. Predictive validity justifies a test's usefulness for making decisions about people—such as selection for a special program. A case is usually made for predictive validity by demonstrating that the instrument correlates well with valid measures of the behavior it is intended to predict.

The credibility of your evaluation depends on the use of valid instruments. Since there is no one established method for determining validity, you do your best in constructing, administering, and interpreting your instruments to anticipate skepticism about your results; you select appropriate methods for investigating possible criticisms; and, finally, you describe the precautions you have taken and the results of your validity investigations in your evaluation report.

Reliability: Does the Instrument Produce Consistent Results?

If you were to give people a math test one day and, without additional instruction, give them the same test two days later, you would expect each student to receive more or less the same score. If this should turn out *not* to be the case, you would have to conclude that your instrument is *unreliable,* because, without instruction, a person's knowledge of math does not fluctuate much from day to day. If the score fluctuates, then, the problem must be with the test. Its results must be influenced by things other than math knowledge. All these other things are called *error. Reliability refers to the extent to which measurement results are free of unpredictable kinds of error.*

Sources of error that affect reliability include:

- Fluctuations in the mood or alertness of respondents because of illness, fatigue, recent good or bad experiences, or other temporary differences among members of the group being measured.
- Variations in the conditions of administration from one testing to the next. These range from various distractions, such as unusual outside noise, to inconsistencies in the administration of the instrument, such as oversights in giving directions.
- Differences in scoring or interpretation of results, chance differences in what an observer notices, and errors in computing scores.
- Random effects by examinees or respondents who guess or check off attitude alternatives without trying to understand them.

Methods for demonstrating an instrument's reliability—whether the instrument is long and intricate or is composed of a single question—involve comparison of one administration with another administration *to the same people.* This is followed by calculation of a correlation coefficient to demonstrate the similarity of the two sets of results. The higher the correlation, the smaller the influence of error. Unlike validity, reliability is usually expressed as a number, a *reliability coefficient,* which is a positive decimal less than 1. Like validity, reliability has a long history, and several methods for demonstrating it have evolved. Which one is used will depend partly on the characteristics of the instrument and partly, as usual, on availability of resources such as money and time.

Test-retest reliability is the oldest and most intuitively obvious method for demonstrating instrument consistency. It involves the basic readministration method described above. Readministration must occur, however, within a time period during which the ability, attitude, or skill cannot itself be expected to change. For measuring most constructs, a good rule-of-thumb has been to wait a month between administrations. Readministration to the same group within a few days or weeks presents a problem: How much of what they remember from the first administration has carried over to the second? Even waiting a month does not eliminate this potential challenge, though it reduces its potency. A long time between administrations, on the other hand, raises the possibility that the *true* skill or attitude of the respondents will have changed. In order to divorce reliability measures from either memory effects or real changes, other methods of detecting reliability have been developed.

Alternate-form reliability attacks the problem of memory effects upon the second administration by having the developer write two essentially equivalent forms of the same instrument.[6] Each individual who receives form A on the first occasion will later receive form B, and vice versa. The method does not completely eliminate the effects of memory, since format across forms remains the same, however, and it does demand that time be spent writing extra items and typing two test forms. In cases where two forms of an instrument have been planned anyway, this kind of check on the reliability of locally produced instruments should be considered.

Split-half reliability[7] yields a measure of test consistency within a single administration. It allows the developer to obtain the two necessary scores from the same group of people by taking two halves of the items comprising an instrument and treating them as two administrations. Thus it separates reliability considerations from the effects of learning or developmental change on the respondents. It compares two forms of the test (the two halves) worked on as simultaneously as is humanly possible! Calculating split-half reliability demands, of course, that the questions that constitute the two halves be alike as possible. Otherwise, your calculation of the effect of error will be complicated by a change in real content.[8] Because of this, the split-half method for estimating reliability is best used with instruments that have many items and where pairs of items can be considered equivalent enough for random distribution to essentially separate forms. These conditions are more likely to be met, say, by items on an instrument with homogeneous items—like a general vocabulary test—than by items on an attitude questionnaire. Then, too, split-half reliability yields a rather specialized sort of information. It tells you whether sub-groups of the items on the test yield essentially the same results. A high split-half correlation means that the test is *internally consistent,* to use the nicely descriptive measurement jargon. Internal consistency, which can be measured in several ways other than split-half correlation, refers to the tendency of different items to elicit the same ability or attitude from any given respondent on a single administration of the instrument. It is important to remember, however, that measures of internal consistency do *not* tell you about error that might result from taking the test on different occasions. For this reason, they are *not* a good way to demonstrate reliability if you need to present a case that the instrument is consistent across administrations.

Inter-rater reliability. Special problems for establishing reliability arise when the "instrument" is actually a *person,* for example, an observer, interviewer, or rater. Such measures that rely on reports of others intro-duce another source of potential error—the person recording. Not only may the test environment and the behavior of the person who is being tested vary from time to time; the perceptions of the person doing the reporting may fluctuate. A rater might, for example, see the same behavior as indicating "strong" enthusiasm at time A, and only "above average" at time B. The best way to demonstrate that your work has been minimally contaminated by inconsistency from "human instruments" is to *use more than one person* to do at least a sample of your interviews or observations. If different people report pretty much the same thing, that is evidence of consistency. For example, if you are using interviews, you should conduct a tryout to verify that two different interviewers questioning the same person come up with the same answers. And when you provide a teacher with a rating scale for the purpose of commenting on the behavior of a student, the instructions and the items should be worded so as to minimize the possibility that another teacher looking at the same behavior might rate it differently.

When observations are used, demonstrate reliability by having a pair of observers watch the same behavioral episodes and then submit their recorded results for comparison. Once you have the data from the two sources, examine these results to assure yourself that the two observers are noticing the same things. The most common way to do this is by calcu-lating a correlation. A high correlation (roughly .70 and above) shows that the measurement method is sufficiently reliable. Lower correlations indi-cate that the observers or reporters do not agree in their reporting, and therefore you should be skeptical of the data you have obtained.

The best method for ensuring high inter-rater reliability, as you might have guessed, is extensive *training and careful instruction* of the people conducting the observations and interviews, or responding to the reports-of-others questionnaire. The problem of inter-rater consistency is diminished when all recorders have learned to use the same set of rules for interpreting the behavior that they witness.

Determining the Reliability of Instruments
Which You Construct Yourself

Determining the reliability of your own measurement instruments amounts essentially to calculating the correlation between different administrations of the instrument or between different items on the instrument at a single administration.

Calculating any correlation coefficient involves setting up the results of various administrations of instruments according to Table 4. You will notice that the columns are labeled X and Y. Column X refers to one administration of an instrument. Column Y refers to another. If you are calculating reliability, X is administration 1, Y is administration 2. (If you were calculating concurrent or predictive *validity,* then X would be the instrument which you were validating, and Y would be the instrument which you were using as a criterion.) Down the left-hand column, you will notice people's names. While you need not refer to people by name, the left-hand column should contain some listing of individuals to whom both administrations have been given. In order to array data for calculating a correlation, simply list the scores on the various measures attained by each person. Then use a standard statistics text to choose the correlation coefficient appropriate to the type of data your instruments have generated.

TABLE 4
Data Display to Begin Calculating
a Correlation Coefficient

Names	X	Y
Evans, E.		
Handler, H.		
Kendall, K.		
Lee, L.		
Norris, N.		
Olsen, O.		
Ryan, R.		
Sanford, S.		
Turner, T.		
Weston, W.		

In circumstances where you anticipate difficulty reducing either X or Y to a single number—for instance where Y, a criterion for estimating concurrent validity, is a set of written reports—consider having judges rank, rate, or categorize them. In these cases, proceed as you would with scores, but be careful to select the appropriate correlation coefficient, one that deals with rankings or categories.

If you are calculating interrater reliability, you will not compare two administrations of the same instrument to the same people; rather you will, in most cases, compare two *judges'* answers to the same item. Down the left-hand column, therefore, you should list *items,* and X should be Observer X's response to the item, Y should be Observer Y's.

If you plan to calculate a reliability coefficient for your own instruments, the following pointers, based on previous experience of test developers, will help you increase the likelihood of obtaining a high coefficient.

Suggestion 1. The circumstances of the reliability study should make possible a high degree of score variability.

This is important because the reliability coefficient depends upon the calculation of a correlation, and the size of the correlation between two measures is affected by the amount of variability in scores on each measure. In other words, if Measure A and Measure B are highly related, the likelihood of demonstrating this relationship is increased if both measures give you scores across a wide range of values. This is true because all measurement is subject to error, and if there is very little difference in the scores of different people (i.e., low variance) on either test, then it only takes a little error to render a person's standing on Measure A very different from her standing on Measure B.

How can you promote a high variance? One thing you can do is to select a large sample of people for your reliability study (from among those who will receive the instrument in actual practice) or, if the sample must be small, find ways to include people whom you would expect to represent both ends of the spectrum of intended respondents as well as the middle of the spectrum, giving you high, medium, and low scores.

High *variability in your sample* helps to increase the chances of demonstrating high reliability in your instrument if indeed it is there. Suppose, for example, you have developed a measure of self-esteem, and you wish to conduct a field trial to determine the test-retest reliability of this instrument. A friend who teaches a group which he reports to be "the most enthusiastic kids I've ever worked with" offers his class to serve as a test sample for your tryout. You administer the test on February 5 and again on March 7. In order to highlight the relative performance of students, let us say that the results of the measure are expressed in rank-order form, and you calculate Spearman's rank-order correlation. Unhappily, you obtain a coefficient of .33—a very low measure of test-retest reliability. What has gone wrong? You examine test results and discover that most of the students on both testings showed high self-esteem. The correlation coefficient that you used compared the rank order of students on the two administrations. As it occurred, the rank of most students differed greatly from the first administration to the second. The student who ranked highest in self-esteem on the first administration ranked eighth on the second administration, and increases and decreases of 5 points in rank, in this class of 23 students, were common. The resulting correlation coefficient was therefore low. Had you administered the instrument to a group of students with wide-ranging differences in self-esteem, you would have been less likely to obtain such a low reliability coefficient. Students who are already very close together on the construct being measured, in this case, self-esteem, are likely to reorder themselves on a subsequent administration owing to unpredictable factors. On the other hand, students whose self-esteem is quite divergent will be more likely to maintain a similar rank order because the unpredictable influences on the score are much smaller than the real, consistent differences in self-esteem among them.

The *size of your sample,* if it is too small, can also be hazardous to your reliability study. If you took the self-esteem measure from the last example and tried it out on a friend's group of six Sunday-school students, for instance, and then readministered it to them five weeks later, your reliability coefficient might be grossly affected by random factors such as some unusual mood or ill health in just a couple of students during one of the two administrations of your instrument.

A second way to increase the variance is to *lengthen the test.* More items on your instrument means a better sample of the construct, and therefore a wider range of possible scores. Suppose, for instance, that the self-esteem measure had ten items, and possible scores could range from 0 to 10. The range of scores you actually obtain may be from 2 to 9 with, say, four-fifths of the respondents scoring from 4 to 8. Upon retesting, a random change for any particular student in answering even one or two questions could seriously change his rank within the group or the position of his score in relation to those of other students.

It is possible, however, to actually reduce the length of a test while increasing its reliability, if you begin with a very long test, choose an appropriate tryout group, and use the tryout results to discover and eliminate the less reliable items (or the less discriminating items, as in item analysis, discussed below in Suggestion 3). Such a procedure does, unfortunately, require additional time and effort and, in some cases, the assistance of a statistician. The number of *response options per question* affects reliability also by restricting or expanding the range of possible scores. You can increase the reliability of an instrument filled with four-option multiple-choice items simply by adding to each a fifth option!

Suggestion 2. If you are calculating split-half reliability, make sure that the two halves are logically parallel.

This will be a consideration only when the items on the test are heterogeneous, measuring different content areas or constructs. In an attitude instrument, for instance, certain items might focus on the respondent's self-image with respect to intelligence, while other items might address self-image with respect to physical appearance. If you need to calculate split-half reliability on such instruments, then, it is best to first classify items according to the construct which they are intended to measure and then randomly assign items from each classification so that each construct will be equally represented on the two halves that are correlated to determine reliability.

Split-half reliabilities, in addition, should be supplemented by a calculation to correct for the smallness of the two item pools being compared. Most statistics texts describe this procedure.

Suggestion 3. As a means of increasing the reliability of your instrument, you can conduct an item analysis for each of the items on it.

The reliability of a particular measurement instrument is affected by the effectiveness of each individual item in discriminating among respondents. The purpose of an item analysis is to point out items that tend to reduce the scores of respondents who score high or to raise the scores of respondents who score low. These items can then be modified or eliminated. The existence of such items reduces reliability because it reduces the variance by narrowing the gap between high and low scorers. Pages 86 to 87 contain suggestions for accomplishing an informal item analysis of in-house constructed measures. This informal analysis is suggested whenever you attempt to develop your own instruments.

Suggestion 4. Try to build the reliability and validity tests into your assessment plan so that they present minimal inconvenience to yourself and the program staff.

If you have little reason to doubt the validity of the instrument, you can use the results from its "official" administration as part of a reliability or validity check. You need not do a separate study. If the attitude measure you are developing is a questionnaire, for instance, you might randomly choose a group of respondents and administer the instrument to this group *twice*—at the time of data collection and three weeks prior or later. The correlation for the random group between these two administrations is your check on *reliability*.

A *validity* study could proceed in much the same way. The criterion measure against which your measure is to be validated—another question-naire, attitude rating scale, or perhaps an observation or a set of written reports—could be administered to a sample of your respondents at roughly the same time as the administration of your instrument.

If your instrument is an observation measure or interview, and you find that you will be using only a *single* reporter, you can estimate this observer's reliability in the following way:

- Videotape or film part of an episode which the observer will be coding.
- Train another person, who will act as a reliability check, to observe in the same way as your observer has been trained. Have this person watch and code the film or videotape. The reliability which you are able to calculate by correlating these two observations will give you an idea of the consistency with which your one observer can be counted on to record accurately the information she sees.

Incidentally, if you are able to have more than one rater observe each event during actual data collection, it is wise to report the *mean* results calculated across these raters in your evaluation report. Such information, because it comes from several sources, is more reliable than separate reports.

Reliability and Attitude Measurement

Some guidance about what constitutes "high" and "low" reliability is in order, since repeated reference is made to them in this chapter. Reliability coefficients of .70 or above are usually considered respectable, regardless of the type of reliability calculated or the method of calculation used, and coefficients of .90 and above are not unusual for standardized achievement tests. In the case of attitude measurements, while reliability coefficients of above .70 are certainly desirable, lower coefficients are sometimes tolerated, although this affects the confidence with which you can make decisions based on measurement results.

The special problems of establishing reliability in the field of attitude measurement should neither be minimized nor exaggerated. It is true that people's attitudes are not, in general, as stable as their skills. Some attitudes fluctuate from day to day. Where this is the case, the standard practice of assessing reliability by taking two measurements a month apart presents problems of interpretation. If the results are different, and if you are without internal consistency data, you do not know whether to attribute these differences to problems in the instrument or to unpredict-able variation in a typical respondent's attitude over time.

If only instruments of doubtful reliability are available to you, consider the amount of time and effort it takes to administer, score, and interpret them, and the amount of inconvenience their administration represents for the respondents. The more resources an instrument demands, the more you should hesitate to use it if its reliability is low. A less reliable instrument is less likely to reveal the real difference that you hope the program makes. On the other hand, if you have the necessary time, and you are not overburdening the respondents, an additional measure might provide you with good hunches about program effects.

Low reliability poses a particular kind of disadvantage for program evaluation. You are using the instruments, after all, to monitor the effectiveness of a program. Typically this means comparing one group mean with another, say, two groups receiving different programs, or the same program at different times. Because the error associated with low reliability is random, that error will tend to affect both administrations. It will *not* systematically bias the results in favor of or against either administration. What low reliability will do is blur the difference between the two group measures. It is as if the instrument were trying to give you a message about program effectiveness, but its low reliability introduced static into your reception. If the message gets through anyway, then the low reliability poses no problem. The difficulty is that when the reliability is low, you may not get the message at all. Your statistical test is more likely to register "no significant difference" as a result of increased variance due to error (as opposed to good variance due to the construct) on each measure. And if this is the result of your study, apologizing for the low reliability of the instrument is likely to sound like Monday-morning quarterbacking—a poor substitute for favorable results.

The need for high test reliability in *program* studies is, however, less crucial than when you are making decisions about individuals. The reason is that statistical bases for *selecting* individuals according to relative standing on a measure are directly related to reliability. In such a situation, you are primarily concerned with purely statistically based predictive validity. In program evaluation, your primary concern is with construct validity and content validity. These, as you have seen, can be demonstrated by methods other than correlations.

Interpreting Validity and Reliability Data About Published Attitude Tests

When you read the manual accompanying an instrument that you might buy, check its presentation of validity and reliability data. Your understanding of such data will help you to interpret your results intelligently for the evaluation audience.

It is hoped that the publisher will provide evidence of *construct* validity, justifying the need for the test and discussing the usefulness of the behaviors it measures as evidence of the presence or absence of attitude constructs. There should be a clear presentation and referencing of the theory or educational practice on which these considerations are based. In addition, the publisher should support a case for validity through descriptions of:

- How items were developed
- The methods and samples used in trying out and revising items
- The types of behaviors that the instrument samples

Also look for references to:

- How the score is related or unrelated to other measures
- Published results of research or evaluation studies that have used the instrument

Whether the publisher provides evidence of content validity or not, you will have to *survey the content of the test items themselves* in order to justify using it to measure your program's objectives. There are three important questions here:

- *How much* of the behavior that you want to measure does the instrument sample?
- In what *proportion* does the instrument represent the various components of what you want to measure?
- To what extent does the instrument measure factors that are *not directly relevant* to what you want to measure?

Concerning the last of these questions, a purchased instrument may contain a sizable minority of items irrelevant to the focus of your evaluation. You may still want to use the measure if you determine that the unwanted items are not numerous enough to interfere with the data obtained from the most relevant items. If you have doubts, you could administer the test as is, but ignore the questionable items when *scoring* the instrument. The existence of some off-the-mark items is not a critical problem, however, if you have obtained positive evidence of internal consistency, such as a high split-half reliability coefficient or favorable item-analysis data. In addition, when you use the publisher's data to defend the quality of the instrument, it may be unwise to modify the instrument by using only those items that appear relevant to your program, since the publisher's case for the usefulness of the instrument is frequently based on the total score.

Some instruments provide scores for *subtests* or subscales as well as an overall score. Publishers may report data concerning the validity and reliability of these subscales as well. In some cases, a subtest will be a discrete section of the instrument; in others, the items of several subscales will be interspersed, making it necessary to consult the scoring key to know which item belongs to which subscale. If you have data, either from your own results or from the publisher's manual, that show low correlations among subscales of an instrument, this is sufficient justification for treating subscale scores separately rather than basing conclusions on the total score.

Please be aware that the empirical information that the publisher provides, whether it pertains to validity or reliability, must be based on samples of respondents who are *like the people you will measure;* otherwise, the results of published studies do not serve as evidence that the instrument will be trustworthy in your situation. In particular, the age range or educational level of your group should be roughly the same as that of the respondents in the published studies.

An instrument characteristic that affects both validity and reliability is the *specificity of procedures* for administering, scoring, and interpreting test results. The validity and reliability of an instrument have meaning only insofar as these procedures remain essentially the same from one administration to another. Thus, the publisher must make these procedures clear. Any departure from them in your situation should be explained, with your conclusions qualified accordingly.

If the instrument involves observer ratings, you will have to calculate inter-rater reliability yourself, since inter-rater reliability is situation specific. It largely depends on how well your observers are trained in using the instrument. This is not evidence that the publisher can give you.

Most published instruments, however, are of the self-report type, and reliability data for them can be useful to you. A publisher may, in fact, compute several reliability coefficients on the basis of one set of test results. You can avoid becoming confused by an abundance of data if you keep in mind that reliability coefficients for self-report instruments refer to either test-retest stability (the extent to which the relative standing of each respondent remains the same on *two separate* occasions) or internal consistency (the extent to which item results are "in tune" with one another). If the reliability coefficient reflects the stability of the test, then the publisher should say how much time elapsed between two administrations and whether the same test or an alternate form was used. If the reliability coefficient reflects the internal consistency of the test, then any of a number of coefficients may have been computed. Reference may be made to split-half, odd-even, KR-20, KR-21, or coefficient-alpha computation procedures; any of these is an acceptable estimate of internal consistency.

Notes

1. If your instrument relies on written reports or observations then the problem of demonstrating validity or reliability boils down to demonstrating *consistency among reporters.* This special case is discussed on page 148 under the topic *inter-rater reliability.*

2. A helpful discussion of concept definition is contained in Chapter 6 of *Measuring the concepts of personality* (Fiske, 1971). The whole book, in fact, is a resource for extending your skills in the field of attitude measurement.

3. Correlations are mentioned often throughout this chapter. Correlation refers to the strength of the relationship between two measures. A high *positive* correlation means that people scoring high on one measure also score high on the other. A *negative* correlation also shows a strong relationship but in the opposite direction. No correlation means that knowing a person's score on one measure does not educate your guess about his score on the other. Correlations are usually expressed by a *correlation coefficient*, a decimal between -1 and +1, calculated from peoples' scores on the two measures. Since there are several different correlation coefficients, each depending on the types of instruments being used, discussion of how to perform correlations to determine validity or reliability is outside the scope of this book. The various correlation coefficients are discussed in most statistics texts however. You might also refer to *How to Analyze Data*, Volume 8 of the *Program Evaluation Kit*.

4. If you are producing a questionnaire where each question addresses unique content, and will therefore be scored and reported individually, worries over each question's contribution to an overall score will not, of course be relevant. Proper numbers of questions and emphasis are nonetheless important, however, and the question-by-question reporting of your results will automatically subject your instrument to scrutiny over appropriateness of content.

5. For an in-depth discussion of methods for systematically breaking down constructs in preparation for testing, see Guttman (1970).

6. This is usually done by writing several versions—as alike as possible—of the same item and then randomly assigning half to each test form.

7. It is nonsense, of course, to consider calculating split-half reliability for instruments where each individual item constitutes an independent measure of different attitude.

8. This necessity, if you think about it, makes split-half reliability similar to alternate-form reliability with both forms administered at the same time.

For Further Reading

Anastasi, A. (1968). *Psychological testing.* New York: Macmillan.

Cronbach, L. J. (1970). Test validation. In R. L. Thorndike (Ed.), *Educational measurement.* Washington, DC: American Council on Education.

Fitz-Gibbon, C. T., & Morris, L. L. (1987). *How to analyze data.* Newbury Park, CA: Sage.

Talmage, H. (1976). *Statistics as a tool for educational practitioners.* Berkeley: McCutchan.

Chapter 12
Summarizing, Analyzing and Displaying the Data

The questionnaires have been returned, the interviews completed, the reports received. You are facing an accumulation of data that you have gone to some lengths to obtain. Now you have the task of organizing the information and extracting the relevant facts. You must expose any response patterns that can help you to determine the degree of success the program has had in achieving its attitude objectives. The suggestions provided by this chapter to help you organize your attitude measurements are aimed at completing the following tasks:

- Recording data on the summary sheet
- Coding and recording open-response data
- Computing results
- Displaying results

Recording Data on the Summary Sheet

The purpose of a data summary sheet is to help you review and work with the entire set of data. Ideally, you should prepare this sheet at the time you design your instrument. Whether you have already collected your data or not, however, the instructions that follow should help you design a data summary form that will serve your needs.

In order to use a data summary sheet, *it is necessary that you have closed-response data or data that have been categorized and coded.* Closed-response data include item results from highly structured observation instruments, interviews, or questionnaires. If, on the other hand, you have item results that are narrative in form, such as from open-ended questions on a questionnaire, interview, or anecdotal observation report, then you will *first* have to categorize and code these responses *if* you wish to use a data summary sheet. Suggestions for coding open-response data appear on page 170.

The first part of the discussion of the use of summary sheets deals with recording and analyzing by hand; the latter part deals with summary sheets for machine scoring and computer analysis.

The Summary Sheet for Scoring by Hand

When scoring by hand, you can choose between two ways of summarizing the data. Your two alternatives are the quick-tally sheet and the people-item roster.

A *quick-tally sheet* displays all response options for each item so that the number of times each option was chosen can be tallied, as in the following examples:

Example

Summary Sheet (quick tally format)

Item #	yes	no	uncertain
1	⊬⊬ IIII	III	II
2	I	⊬⊬ ⊬⊬ II	I

etc.

Questionnaire

yes	no	uncer- tain		
☐	☐	☐	1.	Were the materials available when you needed them?
☐	☐	☐	2.	Were the materials suitable for your group?

Summary Sheet (quick tally format)

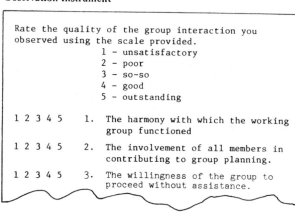

Item #	1 unsatis-factory	2 poor	3 so-so	4 good	5 out-standing
1	|	|		||	⅟ |
2		||	|||	⅟	
3		⅟ ||	|||		

etc.

Observation Instrument

```
Rate the quality of the group interaction you
observed using the scale provided.
                 1 - unsatisfactory
                 2 - poor
                 3 - so-so
                 4 - good
                 5 - outstanding

1 2 3 4 5    1.  The harmony with which the working
                 group functioned

1 2 3 4 5    2.  The involvement of all members in
                 contributing to group planning.

1 2 3 4 5    3.  The willingness of the group to
                 proceed without assistance.
```

The quick-tally sheet allows you to calculate two descriptive statistics for each *group* whose answers are tallied: (1) *the number or percentage of persons who answered each item a certain way,* and (2) *the average response to each item* (with standard deviation) in cases where an average is an appropriate summary. Notice that with a quick-tally sheet, you "lose" the individual person. That is, you no longer have access to individual response patterns. This is perfectly acceptable if all you want to know is how many (or what percentage of the total group) responded in a particular way.

Often, for data summary reasons or *to calculate correlations,* you will need to know about the response patterns of *individuals* within the group. In these cases, a *people-item data roster* will preserve that information. On a people-item data roster the items are listed across the top of the page. The people are listed in a vertical column on the left. They are usually identified by number. Graph paper, or the kind of paper used for computer programming, is useful for constructing these data rosters, even when the data are to be processed by hand rather than by computer. The

people-item data roster below shows the results recorded from the filled-in
questionnaire that follows it:

Example

Summary Sheet (people-item format)

	Item 1	Item 2	Item 3	Item 4	Item 5	Item 6	etc.
Student 1	3	4	4	3	4	4	
Student 2							
Student 3							

etc.

Questionnaire (results for student 1)

Objective: *The child will establish productive and satisfying peer relationships* In the past month:	most of the time 75–100%	often 50–75%	sometimes 25–50%	seldom 0–25%
1. Has at least one or two friends among his classmates	4	3 ✓	2	1
2. Ridicules or teases classmates	1	2	3	4 ✓
3. Is ridiculed or teased by classmates	1	2	3	4 ✓
4. Seeks out classmates to work on projects with him/her	4	3 ✓	2	1
5. Is chosen for activities by classmates	4 ✓	3	2	1
6. Dominates or bullies classmates	1	2	3	4 ✓

The small numerals in the response cells of the questionnaire indicate the
points assigned to each answer for scoring. Unless necessary, they should
not appear on the questionnaire when it is administered to respondents.
Since the items in the above example can go in either direction—a "seldom" response can be a desirable or undesirable response depending on
the item wording—the most desirable response is coded "4" and the least
desirable response is coded "1." Besides permitting you to calculate the
same descriptive statistics as the quick-tally sheet, the people-item data
roster will allow you to compute a total or average score for each person.
It also enables you to use the responses from a few of the items to
calculate an *index* of the strength of a particular attitude, in the same way

you would compute a total score from an attitude rating scale, as described in Chapter 6.

The following example shows a data roster from a team observation study in which three observers took part. The evaluator has chosen to record the scores in such a way as to keep the observers' responses separate from one another. The major interest, however, remains that of obtaining scores for each of the teams. Setting up the summary sheet in this way gives the additional benefit of providing a display for a quick check on interrater reliability, that is, consistency across observers.

Example

Summary Sheet (people-item format)

		Item 1	Item 2	Item 3	etc.
Team 1	Observer 1	4	3	3	
	Observer 2				
	Observer 3				
	AVERAGE				
Team 2	Observer 1				
	Observer 2				
	Observer 3				
	AVERAGE				

etc.

Observation instrument (from observer 1 for team 1)

Rate the quality of the group interaction you observed using the scale provided.

        1 - unsatisfactory
        2 - poor
        3 - so-so
        4 - good
        5 - outstanding

1. The harmony with which the working group functioned.

      1   2   3   (4)   5

2. The involvement of all members in contributing to group planning.

      1   2   (3)   4   5

3. The ability of the group to proceed without outside assistance.

      1   2   (3)   4   5

In the next example, a people-item data roster is used with a rather straightforward questionnaire for parents. The coding, however, poses a special problem.

Example

Summary Sheet (people-item format)

	Item #1	Item #2	Item #3	etc.
Respondent 1	3	2	2	
Respondent 2				
Respondent 3				
Respondent 4				

etc.

Questionnaire (results for respondent 1)

		completely satisfied	satisfied	moderately satisfied	somewhat dissatisfied	completely dissatisfied	unable to judge
		1	2	3	4	5	6
1.	How satisfied were you with your child's progress in reading?			✓			
2.	How satisfied were you with your child's progress in math?		✓				
3.	How satisfied were you with your child's classroom friendships?		✓				

etc.

When you are faced with rows and columns of numbers, the temptation to total or average them sometimes seems irresistible. In this example, say, you might want an average for each respondent and for each item across respondents. However, if you look at the questionnaire, you notice that one of the options, number 6, is different from the others. In selecting options 1, 2, 3, 4, and 5, it is true that as the number gets larger, the degree of dissatisfaction expressed increases. It would therefore be meaningful to sum or average numbers associated with these *five* options in order to get an estimate of the degree of dissatisfaction on a certain item or for a certain respondent. However, using "6" to designate "unable to judge" breaks the pattern set by the other five numbers. That is, a person who checks "unable to judge" is not more dissatisfied than one who checks "completely dissatisfied." Thus, if "6" appears anywhere in the people-item data roster and then averaged with the other numbers, it will inflate the average, causing you to overestimate the dissatisfaction of respondents. Be careful to omit "other" options when you average results.

The Summary Sheet for Computer Analysis

If a computer will analyze your data, then your data summary task will likely involve coding responses in preparation for data entry.[1] Sometimes questionnaires can be formatted so that the data can be read and recorded directly from the questionnaire into the computer. Often, however, coding sheets are used to set up a file of your results, usually following the format of the people-item data roster; each row usually represents one individual's responses.

Data for the computer are recorded from coding sheets onto cards, tape, or disks in a format defined by a *codebook* written by the data analyst. Data coding onto cards is accomplished by punching holes over the numbers in the 80 card columns. The computer reads the holes in the cards electronically. The printing seen along the top of the card is for the *user* to read, not the machine. When there is information to fill more than 80 columns, a second card is simply inserted behind the first in the data deck.

The example below shows a card which has been punched to record the results of a school attitude questionnaire for one student. The example shows the *coding sheet* entries which the operator followed when key punching and the *codebook* which specified the meaning of each column on the data card. Coding sheets of this sort can be purchased from any large stationery dealer.

Example. An evaluator has administered a 20-item questionnaire dealing with high school students' assessment of the relevance of a district's vocational education program to their life goals. The questionnaire is the pretest in a year-long study comparing *two* new programs, A and B, with the district's usual program. The three programs have been installed in each of the district's four high schools.

All data relevant to the study will be punched onto cards for computer analysis. The data card here represents *one* student taking part in the evaluation.

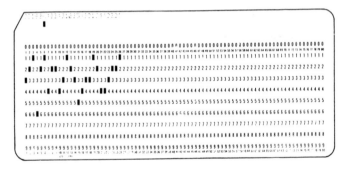

The keypunch operator produced the card according to the numerals entered into the appropriate columns on a coding sheet. Coding sheet entries which correspond to this card appear below:

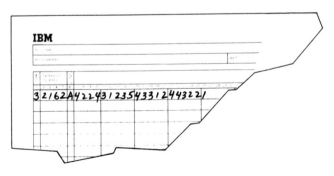

The meaning of the numerals has been determined by the following codebook.

Column	Variable	Variable Name	Range of Values	Value Labels
1	School	SCHL	1-4	1=Washington 2=Jefferson 3=Reed 4=Kennedy
2	Classroom	CLSS	1-6	---
3-4	Student ID#	ID	1-50	---
5	Student sex	SEX	1-2	1=male 2=female
6	Program	PGM	A,B,C	A=Experimen- tal Pgm. A B=Experimen- tal Pgm. B C=Control (usual program)
7-26	Item-by-item responses to school attitude questionnaire taken Sept. 6	ATTITUDE	1-5	

The codebook can be read as follows:

Column numbers refer to the 80 columns on the card. Each column can hold only one digit, letter, or symbol. Column 1 is a school code. Columns 7 through 26 represent the respondent's answers to each questionnaire item. Column 7 represents Item #1, column 8 represents Item #2, and so forth.

Variable and *Variable Name.* Each piece of information is called a variable. A short name is given each variable for use in the computer. It is common practice to choose variable names that are mnemonic.

Range of Values. Each variable will have different values for different cases. Here there are four schools designated value 1 through 4, and three programs valued A, B, and C. (Note that since these symbols name categories and are not numbers to be manipulated, they can be either letters or numbers.) For each of the 20 items on the questionnaire (variable name: ATTITUDE), the respondent has five options, so *each item value* ranges from 1 to 5.

A reference to the codebook shows that the person represented by the card is a student at school 3, Reed, in classroom 2, whose ID number is 16. The student is male (sex 2) and a member of Experimental Program A. Responses on items 1 through 3 of the questionnaire were 4, 2, and 2, respectively.

If you have not yet solidified the format of your instrument, you might want to *set up your questionnaire or recording form so that data can be directly keypunched from it.* Such a questionnaire simply specifies, in a conspicuous place, which of the 80 columns of the card any particular response will occupy and the value to be punched for each response option provided. The example below shows such a questionnaire.

Example

Tutoring Project
Teacher's Questionnaire

1. (20-22) Approximately how many pupils were you teaching at the time of the program? _____

2. (23-25) a. How many pupils usually received tutoring on any one day? _____

   (26) b. What were pupils who were not receiving tutoring doing while the tutoring was in progress? Please check one box indicating the usual situation.

   1☐ All pupils were usually tutored so this question does not apply.

   2☐ The situation varied too much to state a "usual" situation.

   3☐ Working in class on academic subjects

   4☐ Working in class on non-academic subjects

   5☐ Other (please specify)_____ (27)

3. (28-30) a. Approximately what was the total number of your pupils who received tutoring at some time during the program? _____

   b. In each of the following boxes, please indicate approximately how many of the pupils who received tutoring:

   · were eager to be tutored at first   [   ] (31-33)
     and stayed eager.

   · were eager to be tutored at first   [   ] (34-36)
     but then lost interest.

   · were reluctant to be tutored at   [   ] (37-39)
     first but then enjoyed it.

   · were reluctant to be tutored at   [   ] (40-42)
     first and did not enjoy it.

4. (43-45) What activities, if any, did students have to give up in order to tutor?

   _____   DO NOT WRITE IN THIS SPACE
   _____   ☐ ☐   (43)
   _____   E   A
   _____   ☐ ☐ ☐   (44)
   _____   BS AF PM
   _____   ☐ ☐   (45)
                               R   V

This questionnaire displays several varieties of questions whose answers can be directly keypunched:

Apparently columns 1 through 19 on the computer card to be punched will be taken up by teacher, school, and program identification. Questionnaire answers are encoded beginning with column 20.

Columns 20, 21, and 22 are reserved for the number of students in the teacher's class. This number will be directly punched.

The number of students tutored in a single day is recorded in columns 23-35. Again, the operator will punch in the number written by the teacher.

Column 26 records the teacher's response to a multiple-choice question. The number of the box checked by the teacher will be keypunched. If box 5 (other) is checked, an additional notation must be punched in column 27. The keypunch operator can be given a codebook that classifies all possible responses to this question and indicates a code to be entered into column 27 to represent the types of answers given.

Columns 28 through 30 again record a number that the teacher is required to write in, as do columns 31 through 42. Note that care has been taken here to place the column numbers close to the place on the page where the response will be made. This should cut down on possible keypunch errors caused by having to glance across a page *The numbers of the punchcard columns should appear on the questionnaire as close as possible to the place where the response appears.*

Columns 43 through 45 are taken up by the codes for an open-ended question. Apparently this is a question that the data analyst has decided must be *precoded* before the questionnaire is given to the keypunch operator. Someone trained to reduce the answers to code form will read the answers to question 4 and check the boxes in the shaded section labeled "Do not write in this space." The answer will be interpreted according to three characteristics:

- Column 43 will record whether the activity the tutor has given up is extracurricular (E) or academic (A).
- Column 44 records whether it is one with objectives that are primarily basic skills (BS), affective (AF), or psychomotor (PM).
- Column 45 encodes whether these missed activities are required (R) or voluntary (V).

Punching directly from the questionnaire makes it imperative that a codebook defining the columns be provided for the keypunch operator. The codebook will give the keypunch operator a question-by-question guide for such eventualities as "no response," omitted or improperly entered data, and special instructions about what to do with "other" and "specify" responses.

Coding and Recording Open-Response Data

Working with open-response data requires that you develop a system for *categorizing* the information and reducing it to a form that can be looked at all at once and summarized. You can analyze the information gathered in one of two ways: (1) you can produce a purely descriptive written summary, or (2) you can assign numerical values to different types of responses and use this data in further statistical analyses. Which you choose will depend on your purposes.

For many evaluation reports, all you will want is an anecdotal summary paragraph. If so, your goal will be to detect the most frequently expressed opinions, and to include these in your report, directly quoting when possible. Directions for analyzing open-response data for such a descriptive summary appear in Chapter 8 under the heading "Summarizing a large number of written reports," and an example of reporting frequency counts from open-ended responses appears at the very end of this chapter.

If you decide to encode open responses into *numerical* or more precise categorical form, you can then use this summary in more detailed data analyses. Suppose, for example, you asked 100 teachers to describe their experiences at a Teacher Learning Center where they received in-service training in classroom management techniques. After reading their reports, and summarizing them for reporting in paragraph form, you wonder how teachers' opinions of the Teacher Center might be related to their own felt needs for better classroom management skills. You can find this out by categorizing teachers into, say, five opinion levels—very favorable toward the training experience, through so-so, to very unfavorable—giving each teacher an opinion score, 1 through 5. A similar categorization could be made to rate teachers according to how much they felt a need to improve their classroom management. Such rank-order data enable you to calculate a correlation coefficient either by hand or by computer.

Time spent in categorizing open-response data can yield useful information, although the difficulty of the task will vary from one situation to another. Precise instructions for arriving at your categories and summarizing your data cannot be provided, but the following advice should help make your task more manageable:

1. Since you are working with attitudinal information, it is likely the data will represent a set of opinions or attitudes that range from positive to negative. If you are working with on-site observations, the data will represent a set of behaviors that range from desirable to undesirable. Read what you consider to be a representative sampling of the data (about 25%) and determine if it is possible to begin with three general categories—(a) clearly favorable or desirable, (b) clearly unfavorable or undesirable, and (c) those in between.

2. If the data can be divided into these three piles, you can then put aside for the moment those in categories (a) and (b) and proceed to refine category (c) by dividing it into three piles:

   • those that are more favorable than unfavorable
   • those that are more unfavorable than favorable
   • those in between

3. Refine categories (a) and (b) as you did (c). If you cannot divide them into three attitude gradations, then use two; or if the initial breakdown seems as far as you can go, leave it as is.

4. Have one or more people check your categories. This can be done by asking others to go through a similar categorization process or to critique the categories you selected.

Performing Calculations with Attitude Data

Computing Results Person-by-Person

You will want to analyze attitude results in terms of how *particular people* responded in one of two situations:

1. You may want to make statements in your report on the nature of "People who responded K tended to J," where K is expression of a particular attitude, and J is another attitude, a behavior, or perhaps a level of achievement.

   This can be done in two ways:

   a. use questionnaire responses (K) to *classify* people, and then calculate an average J per group, or
   b. *correlate* K with J.

   In either case, you will be able to answer questions such as "Do people who respond to one question in a particular way tend to respond to another question in a consistent way?" "Will customers who state a preference for informative labels also tend to have high incomes?" "Are different results associated with recognizable groups of respondents? For example, how much does dissatisfaction with the school's academic program vary with grade level, sex, parents' level of education, ethnic origin, or SES?" Before you bother to compute a statistic, of course, you should be clear about the question you are trying to answer, and consider who would be interested in the answer and what impact the answer might have.

2. You may want to calculate concurrent or predictive validity or reliability of the instrument via a correlation.

In either of these cases, you have several choices of what to use for K (and J, if it is an indication of an attitude). You can characterize people's attitudes in one of the three ways mentioned often throughout this book:

- In terms of each individual's response to a single item. As has been mentioned, sorting people according to responses to a single item usually carries low credibility because of the poor reliability of single answers. If classification of people is critical to the evaluation, you should probably use multiple measures, an index, or an attitude rating scale to achieve it.

- According to an *index* depicting an attitude or behavioral tendency which you have computed on the basis of responses to several items. Use of such an index is discussed in Chapter 5.

- According to an *attitude rating scale*. This sort of instrument, developed according to a technique outlined in Chapter 6, produces a single attitude score per person which carries high credibility, lends itself easily to scrutiny in terms of reliability and validity, and can be used in data summarization in exactly the same way achievement scores can be used.

Computing Results for Item-by-Item Interpretation

The number of possible calculations and tabulations that can be performed with responses to attitude items is legion, particularly if you have access to calculators or a computer. They are beyond the scope of this book, and you should consult a book on data analysis and reporting for more detailed instructions.[2] For the purpose of summarizing responses to individual items, the discussion here presents some statistics—totals, percentages, and group averages.

In some instances, computation will involve nothing more than adding tallies:

Example. Of the 50 people interviewed, 19 men and 13 women reported having taken part in the company recreation program. These 32 people reported having engaged in the following activities:

	men	women	total
handball	19	7	26
lifting weights	16	12	28
team games	17	10	27
swimming	12	12	24
aerobics classes	8	8	16
jogging	10	8	18

In other cases, you may want to convert the numbers to percentages and report both totals and percentages:

Example. Of the 500 questionnaires mailed to the parents, 225 were returned. The following presents the numbers and percentages of responses item by item:

		Yes	Uncertain	No
1.	Have you been given an explanation of why most classes at school consist of more than one grade level?	137 (61%)	26 (12%)	62 (27%)
2.	Are you in favor of class-room groupings that consist of children of more than one grade level?	170 (75%)	15 (7%)	40 (18%)
3.	Are you in favor of having parent volunteers in your child's classroom?	220 (98%)	3 (1%)	2 (1%)

To obtain the percentage answering "yes" in the above example, the number of "yes" responses was divided by the total number of responses, and then multiplied by 100. Thus:

$$\frac{\text{number of "yes" responses to \#1}}{\text{total number of responses}} = \frac{137}{(137+26+62)} = \frac{137}{225} = 0.61$$

$$0.61 \times 100 = 61\%$$

If answers to the questions on your instrument represent a progression, for example, degrees of an attitude, you may wish to obtain a *group average* for the responses to each question. Suppose you asked 25 people this question:

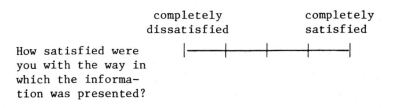

How satisfied were you with the way in which the information was presented?

You could then calculate a group average for the item by the following procedure:

1. Assign a scale value to each point on the continuum:

2. Tally the number of responses for each point on the continuum. On the item:

> 5 people responded "1"
> 7 people responded "2"
> 7 people responded "3"
> 2 people responded "4"
> 4 people responded "5"
> _____
> 25 Total

3. Multiply the number of responses times the value of the responses and add the results.

> 5 x 1 = 5
> 7 x 2 = 14
> 7 x 3 = 21
> 2 x 4 = 8
> 4 x 5 = 20
> _____
>   68

4. Divide the number obtained on the previous step by the total number of responses.

$$68 \div 25 = 2.72$$

This is the *average* (mean) response to the item for the group of 25 people. It shows a tendency slightly to the "dissatisfied" side of the middle.

By *averaging* group scores on a set of items, you are reducing or summarizing the data in order to make them easier to work with and interpret. The summarized data can then be graphed and displayed. Should you wish to submit the data to statistical tests to look for statistically significant differences between groups, for example, average group responses will enable you to do so.

There is, however, one easily recognized situation in which a group average score may be misleading and should *not* be used. Suppose, for example, that on a given question, the responses pile up at the two *ends* of the continuum. People's opinions seem to be polarized. To report such results as an average would fail to reflect this polarization, and would therefore mislead the audience.

Example. On the following scale, responses were distributed as indicated by the numbers below the scale.

	strongly disagree	dis- agree	un- certain	agree	strongly agree
	1	2	3	4	5

Scale	1	2	3	4	5
Number of respondents	20	6	2	2	24

Were you to calculate the average response, you would obtain 3.07, close to "uncertain." Since 20 people checked "strongly disagree" and 24 checked "strongly agree," it would certainly be misleading to report only that the average response was 3.07, "uncertain"! The *bimodal* character of the responses would have to be reported.

Displaying Item-by-Item Results

If you have used a questionnaire, you might wish to display the results *on the questionnaire itself.* Given sufficient space on a blank questionnaire, you could record the number of percentage of each response option:

	Yes	No
Did you attend the open house?	☐ 200 (67%)	☐ 100 (33%)
Did you attend the Christmas party?	☐ 151 (50%)	☐ 149 (50%)

If you have used continuum or Likert-type questions to measure degrees of an attitude and have arrived at an average score for each question, the procedure varies slightly for displaying results on the instrument. In this situation, you should place a mark at the *average score* and then connect the marks with a line:

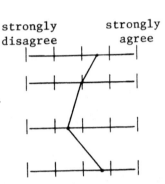

1. I like school a lot.

2. I like school better this year than last year.

3. I think my teacher likes me.

4. I get along with my classmates.

If you are working with results from *two* groups, you might want to plot *both* sets of results on the same questionnaire, possibly using a solid line for one and a dotted line for the other. Thus you would have a good picture of where the differences occur. Looking at the data in this way might help you to decide where you should look (such as item #3) for important factors that differentiate groups or programs.

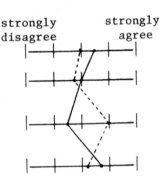

1. I like school a lot.

2. I like school better this year than last year.

3. I think my teacher likes me.

4. I get along with my classmates.

Program X Group ————
Program Y Group - - - - - -

If you want to display the frequency with which certain statements or observations were made in a set of reports, observation records, or open-ended replies, this can be done in table form. With such open-response data, you begin by underlining key statements from each respondent. After you count recurrent observations or opinions, results can be displayed as below.

Example

> 10. If there is something on your mind not covered by the questionnaire--either something you are especially pleased with or something you are concerned about--please let us know by writing in this space and on the back of the page.

Your evaluation report concerning this item would include this section:

> In their responses to Item 10, N (total #) people expressed the following categories of criticisms:
>
> | criticism | number of people expressing criticism |
> | --- | --- |
> | parents were not advised of the objectives of the program | 5 |
> | parents felt they were asked to attend meetings only to satisfy funding requirements and not to take part in the program planning process | 4 |
> | etc. | |

Notes

1. Basic texts containing additional information on data processing are available, One such book is Feingold's *Introduction to Data Processing* (1975).

2. Two other books in the *Program Evaluation Kit* address these topics: *How to Analyze Data* (Volume 8) and *How to Communicate Evaluation Findings* (Volume 9).

Appendix A:

Names and Addresses of Publishers of Attitude Measures

AP	Academic Press 111 - 5th Avenue New York, New York 10003
CED	Center for Educational Development University of Minnesota Minneapolis, Minnesota 55455
Co	M. V. Covington Department of Psychology University of California Berkeley, California 94720
CPS	Center for Psychological Services Columbia Medical Building, Suite 419 1835 Eye Street N.W. Washington, D.C. 20006
Cr	Virginia C. Crandall Section of Motivated Behavior Fels Research Institute Yellow Springs, Ohio 45387
CRT	Counselor Recordings and Tests Box 6184, Acklen Station Nashville, Tennessee 37212
CTB	CTB McGraw-Hill Del Monte Research Park Monterey, California 93940

DFP	The Devereux Foundation Foundation Press Devon, Pennsylvania 19333
Du	James Dunn American Institute for Research P.O. Box 1113 Palo Alto, California 94302
EIP	Educational Improvement Program 2010 Campus Drive Duke University Durham, North Carolina 27706
ERIC	Educational Document Reproduction Service Box 190 Arlington, Virginia 22210
ESD	Educational Skills Development, Inc. 179 East Maxwell Street Lexington, Kentucky 40508
ETS	Tests in Microfiche/Test Collection Educational Testing Service Princeton, New Jersey 08540
HMC	Hahnemann Medical College and Hospital of Philadelphia Department of Mental Health Sciences Research and Evaluation Services 314 North Broad Street Philadelphia, Pennsylvania 19102
HM	Houghton-Mifflin Company 777 California Avenue Palo Alto, California 94304
IPAT	Institute for Personality and Ability Testing Inc. P. O. Box 188 1602 Coronado Dr. Champaign, IL 61820
	Department of Educational Psychology City University of New York 33 West 42nd Street New York, New York 10036

LHP	London House Press 1550 N. Northwest Highway Park Ridge, Illinois 60068
Mc	Dr. Lawrence McCluskey Institute of Administrative Research Box 301, Teachers College Columbia University 525 West 120 Street New York, New York 10027
No	Dr. S. Nowicki Department of Psychology Emory University Atlanta, Georgia 30322
OI	Ontario Institute for Studies in Education Publication Sales 252 Bloor Street West Toronto, Ontario M5S 1V6
PAA	Paul S. Amidon Associates 4329 Nicollet Avenue South Minneapolis, Minnesota 55409
PC	Psychological Corporation 757 Third Avenue New York, New York 10017
PUBS	Purdue University Book Store 360 State Street West Lafayette, Indiana 47906
SEI	Self Esteem Institute 1736 Stockton Street San Francisco, California 94133
SRA	Science Research Associates 155 N. Wacker Drive Chicago, Illinois 60606
SUP	Stanford University Press Stanford, California 94305
VPR	Vocational Psychology Research N620 Elliott Hall University of Minnesota Minneapolis, Minnesota 55455

Wa	Walter B. Waetjen Cleveland State University Cleveland, Ohio 44115
Wr	L. S. Wrightsman George Peabody College for Teachers Box 508 Nashville, Tennessee 37203

References

Campbell, D. A., & Fiske, D. W. (1959). Validation by the multitrait multimethod matrix. *Psychological Bulletin, 56*, 81-105.

Christie, R., et al. (1970). *Studies in Machiavellianism.* New York: Academic Press.

DiVesta, F. (1965). Developmental patterns in the use of modifiers as modes of conceptualization. *Child Development, 36*, 185-213.

Edwards, A. L., & Porter, B. C. (1972). Attitude measurement. In *The affective domain* (pp. 107-125). Washington, DC: National Special Media Institutes, The Gryphon House.

Feingold, C. (1975). *Introduction to data processing.* Dubuque, IA: Wm. C. Brown.

Fiske, D. W. (1971). *Measuring the concepts of personality.* Chicago: Aldine.

Gronlund, N. E. (1959). *Sociometry in the classroom.* New York: Harper & Brothers.

Guttman, L. (1970). Integration of test design and analysis. In *Proceedings of the 1969 Invitational Conference on Testing Problems* (pp. 53-65). Princeton, NJ: Educational Testing Service.

Index

NOTES